*For My Wife Cyndee*

*And Our Children*

*Evan, Emma, Maddie and Lily*

*And to all Vietnam Veterans*

*Welcome Home*

# TABLE OF CONTENTS

# 1

# THE GENERAL

Imagine my surprise. White House Chief of Staff John Kelly stopped me in my tracks in a press briefing not long ago. The former Marine General was discussing his new role in the White House when he dropped in a little shocker. He said he liked his new job but the best job he ever had was many years ago when he was an infantry sergeant.

What did you just say? Do my ears deceive me? I had to laugh because fifty years ago I was an infantry sergeant in Vietnam. It wasn't the best job I ever had. It was the worst job I ever had, and if you read this book you'll probably agree with me. At the time I described it as the worst job in the world.

We slogged through steaming, swampy rice paddies filled with leeches and snakes. We were relentlessly set upon by mosquitos, fire ants and near lethal bees. Our backs were bent by heavy ammunition-filled packs and in my case a cumbersome, top-heavy radio. Our feet were scabbed over by immersion foot. We chained smoked. We traversed the Mekong Delta waters on landing craft called Tango boats. We flew air mobile missions on helicopters called Hueys. We would trek days on end eating horrible and insufficient food called C-Rations. If there was time, we even complained about our lack of opportunity to contract venereal diseases.

The local people we were there to liberate detested us. Sure, they would trade us sickly, sweet Vietnamese Coca-Cola for our discarded C-Ration meals but mostly they tried to kill us. We looked at every tree as a potential sniper nest and every trail as a potential home for a trip-wire grenade, a toe-popper, a Claymore mine or even a so-called Bouncing Betty that would pop up and cut you in half so fast you only had one brief moment to realize you were dead. They ambushed us, harassed us, sent mortar rounds into our base camps and generally prevented us from ever getting a good night's sleep.

Best job ever? I think not. And it gets worse. An infantry sergeant has to make decisions, often under duress, often with too little information, that can have life and death consequences for the very people he serves with intimately every day. Buddies, friends, teammates, call them what you will but the bottom line is that the stakes were high and the outcomes were very personal.

It was a tall order for an immature twenty-year old like me. I had smoked too much dope, flunked out of college, lost my draft deferment and ended up in this living hell. Trying to keep people alive became that extra layer of pressure that defined my time in Vietnam. It is an understatement to say I grew up fast and got serious in a hurry. Most of us got home. Those who did not are still mourned.

It was an often told lie to say those who did not make it home died for their country, or more to the point, their countrymen. By 1968, a majority of Americans hated Vietnam, hated the leaders who sent us there and increasingly hated us for fighting the war. Only our families, friends and fellow soldiers cobbled together a faithful support system that prevented us from being totally abandoned by the country we loved and left behind. Our only real motivation was simple.

Survival.

I was among the most fortunate survivors. After Vietnam I went to good schools, had great jobs and with my wife of thirty years produced a loving family. Surviving Vietnam put an invisible chip on my shoulder I carry to this day to drive me to certain levels of achievement. I found an occupation, television journalism, perfectly suited to someone with my short attention span and healthy disrespect for authority. For the last thirty-five years of my professional life I ran big city television newsrooms topping out as the General Manager at WJLA-TV, the ABC affiliate in Washington D.C., where I had roughly 300 employees.

I was a leader and I must have been reasonably good at it because people kept hiring me to do these jobs. But what kind of leader was I? The answer fascinated me when I figured it out quite by accident. It came from a very casual conversation at work a few years back when someone was asking me about leadership philosophy, leadership guidelines and how I had the confidence to make quick decisions under pressure on difficult issues.

I thought about it for a moment and without much deep consideration I said the damnedest thing.

"I learned everything I needed to know about leadership as a 20 year-old Infantry Sergeant in Vietnam."

Nobody was as shocked as I was when that popped out of my mouth but as I thought more about it I came to believe the accuracy of the statement.

Where better to learn to be decisive under pressure?

Where better would I learn under stress to be uncomfortably honest, fair and inclusive?

Where better would I learn the value of teamwork and what I always called casting, making sure the right people were in the right jobs?

And above all else, where better but forged in battle would I learn to always, always look out for my people?

So maybe General Kelly and I weren't all that far off after all. It doesn't matter if it was the best job or the worst job you ever had. It was the job that defined you, shaped your character and prepared you for the challenges ahead in life.

In this book you will see how events in Vietnam shaped my thinking and how my opinion of what was going on evolved over my time there. I have left out much of the blood and gore battle descriptions common to war memoirs. You can read that between the lines and get a good sense of it from the letters I wrote home to my mom that provide something of a time line for this narrative.

Here's fair warning. I was not a gung ho soldier. I was a draftee counting the days to my trip home. I never took unnecessary chances. I was only committed to doing whatever I could to keep our team safe and to avoid as many casualties as possible.

Another warning. This whole project started when my sister and wife found all the old letters I had sent home to my mother from Vietnam. They are excerpted throughout. My mom and I weren't even on the best of terms. I called her by her first name, Lucy, and not out of any great respect. She drank way too much and embarrassed me often. But in Vietnam I reverted to calling her mom. And throughout that awful time she became my lifeline.

# 2

# BASIC TRAINING

RAW MEAT, SAY HELLO TO the U.S. Army.

The shouting started before we were even off the bus. The Army had painted rows of foot prints at the bus stop in something like a military formation. They wanted each one of us to stand on a set of those foot prints. And they wanted us there fast. Imagine fifty or so nervous guys trying to play what amounted to musical chairs as Star Trooper-like army sergeants screamed at us. The intimidation started right then.

Dumb ass, recruits. Maggots. Numbnuts. Shit for Brains. Jerkoffs. The list was endless and they came up with new ones almost every day to come.

And this was long before the age of political correctness so were we also pussies, faggots, queers, lepers and retards. And, of course, we were treated to the first half dozen or so of what would end up being at least a hundred ways to pronounce the word motherfucker.

There was endless talk about what it would take to survive in "this man's army." That phrase never made sense to me. Who was that man? What was it about his army? These were questions I was just wise enough not to ask.

Soon enough our heads were shaved, our civilian clothes were replaced and our individuality was placed on the chopping block. We were herded to a dark, damp barracks to await our fate.

Very early, like 5am early, the next day we met our drill

instructor. He was a vision of military perfection. He stood straight and tall, his shoes reflected every light bulb in the building, his uniform was pressed to the nines and he was extremely put out to be in our presence. He let that be known very quickly.

"Drop your cocks and grab your socks," became his usual wakeup call. "This is where you learn if you can find your ass in the dark with both hands."

That morning he took a few extra moments to explain to us that we were all scum. We were lower than whale shit in the ocean. And somehow, against all the odds, he was going to transform "every last swinging dick in the room" into a proud, combat ready soldier. He also pointed out that he would do his absolute best to make us all hate him before it was over.

But it was hard to hate drill instructors. They were such characters. They were funny. They were total bullies but amazing comics at the same time. And you couldn't laugh or you would be doing pushups forever. I've heard a lot of speakers in my lifetime but some of the best speeches ever were from drill instructors dressing down ragtag assemblies of frightened recruits. They loved to pick out one guy and insult him.

I remember one sergeant during basic training at Ft. Lewis who got right up in a terrified kid's face.

"Cosgrove, I think you're a pervert," he said. "And I want you to know that when you piss in my latrine you are only allowed to shake your dick twice. You shake it a third time that's playing with yourself and I'll have you hauled off to the stockade. Do you understand me?"

The poor kid looked like he might pee his pants at that very moment.

"Yes, sir."

"Don't ever call me sir. That's for officers."

"Yes, Sergeant."

"How many shakes, Cosgrove?

"Two, sir."

"WHAT?"

"Two, Sergeant."

It took real talent to insult these kids, rip them to shreds, make them cry and then make us all laugh at the same time. They were masters of hilarious phrasing, impeccable timing and ruthless sarcasm. And somehow the result was a bunch of recruits all thinking the drill sergeant walked on water.

"Johnson you are dumb like a hammer. When I said turn left I didn't mean take three rights. I meant left, numbnuts. Tell me, did your mama have any kids that lived?"

"Jones, your girlfriend must be the saddest person on her block. You are hung like a hamster."

Or my personal favorite.

"Smith, I want you to grab your left ear with your right hand. Now I want you to grab your right ear with your left hand. Now, pull your head out of your ass and get this RIGHT!"

One last one I did not hear but read about somewhere along the way was when a drill instructor walked up to a group of soldiers misbehaving in some way or another.

"Soldiers, what in the name of Hindu butt sex is going on here?"

In the end, this talk kept us entertained to some degree as we learned how to fire rifles, throw hand grenades and march endlessly. It was called close order drill and for hours every day we marched in formation. We turned left in unison. We double-timed in unison. We halted in unison. In the eyes of the military we essentially were being programmed to work as a group and to follow orders. I think there was some belief that if we all followed orders often enough on the parade grounds we would be willing to charge a machine gun nest if we were ordered to do that in the future.

I could have saved us all a lot of trouble. Not many draftees I knew planned to charge machine gun nests.

Not many draftees planned on being army officers either but early on I was faced with an odd choice. I had tested in to Officer Candidate School which would mean adding a year of military service. I had volunteered for the draft because it was a two-year commitment rather than the three-year deal most people agreed to with an ordinary enlistment. Did I want to add a year of service in exchange for a big advancement in rank?

I write in total disbelief that I ever even considered such a thing.

The end of my time at Ft. Lewis was marked by indecision. I received a start date to attend Officers Candidate School and then declined to sign the papers that would have kept me in the Army an additional year. Looking back, let's say wisely declined. I had learned being a Second Lieutenant wasn't all that desirable, anyway. They were considered, fairly or not, the most dangerous people in Vietnam. They had a high casualty rate. It was often said that long after soldiers should have reacted instantly a Second Lieutenant would still be standing up trying to read a map. Regardless, in my case it was an extra year I did not want to give up.

In Vietnam, in my view, there was an interesting division between officers and enlisted men. The officers wanted to please their superiors. They made many decisions based on the values of those superiors. Enlisted men had a much different view. We wanted to survive. We made our decisions based on what would keep us alive. There was plenty of cross over from time to time but by and large that was the case. What was the first priority? Was it a military objective or keeping your head down? More on this later.

After dropping OCS and then doing everything I could to avoid being a medic, I was temporarily a soldier without an assignment. I had a date for a new infantry training class three weeks out so the Army did something I could not believe. They kept me at the Basic Training School at Ft. Lewis to help the drill sergeants. And get this. They put temporary stripes on my arm and called me an "Acting Jack" sergeant.

So let's review this little mind boggler. After eight whole weeks in the army I was now put in charge of entire platoons of new recruits when the "real" sergeants had time off. Don't be bothered by youth and inexperience. I had stripes on my arms and now I was expected to call guys maggots and dirt bags. Within just a few short hours I learned to excel at random insults. I'm pleased to report I took to it instantly. I could make a recruit seize up with the best of them. It was an exercise in the raw abuse of power and I don't recall being too offended by it. Heck, I was enjoying myself.

"Drop and give me twenty-five, soldier!"

"Salute that fencepost, trooper."

"Wipe that tear from your eye, boy."

I know it sounds awful but most of it was good natured and having been on both sides of that little festival of verbal torment I can assure you the death count was zero. But what a life lesson I learned in those short weeks.

Grown men actually trembled in front of me because I was wearing those silly stripes. I was a weedy kid who looked sixteen years old. Many of these guys were older, smarter, larger and far more accomplished than I was. But they didn't really see me at all. They saw those stripes, those symbols of authority. They reacted involuntarily in the circumstance and were as submissive as I had been a few short weeks earlier. But the lesson for me was simple. Don't be submissive in later life. Don't let authority figures have that edge. Bosses, cops, ushers and all manner of people will use symbols of authority to get their way. Sometimes they will get their way, but never accept intimidation based on those symbols.

I then quickly moved on to Advanced Infantry Training. I found myself with about thirty guys from the New York National Guard. Most of them were from the New York City area. I swear they had been sent from Central Casting. They were native New York City kids who seemed to end every sentence with "you got a problem with that?" They were profane, verbally combative and funny as hell. They had a motto I ended up adopting as my own.

"Fuck 'em if they can't take a joke!"

As in, "Those pedestrians had to scatter when I drove through that crosswalk. Fuck 'em if they can't take a joke."

Or, "Of course we ate all the pizza before that other platoon got there. Fuck 'em if they can't take a joke.

My thanks to the New York National Guard for providing me with a slogan that worked so well in my journalism career later in life.

All the bosses are upset because your story offended a bunch of advertisers.

"Fuck 'em if they can't take a joke"

The National Guard guys all admitted they were there to avoid Vietnam. I thought for me it was unavoidable. Imagine my surprise when I got orders to report to Berlin, Germany.

Berlin was amazing. And I was assigned to what might have

been the best duty in the Army at that point. Several of us were selected be part of some honor guard unit at the American Head-quarters Compound. We suffered the indignity of checking the ID's of young, pretty German girls arriving for work in the morning. We rode with the State Department guys out on to the runway at Templehof Airport to load the diplomatic pouches on to planes bound for Washington D.C. At one point we even got to spend two weeks as prison guards at the fabled Spandau Prison where all the Nazi war criminals were held. When we were there only one prisoner remained, Rudolf Hess who at one point was Hitler's Deputy Fuhrer.

They even gave us full time passes to hang around all the crazy bars in downtown Berlin.

But something was happening during these months. As much fun as it was, I was constantly aware that the major global event of my generation was taking place halfway around the world while I sipped beer out of a glass boot at the Old Eden Club.

The Army was amazingly accommodating when I wandered in one day and volunteered to go to Vietnam. I was granted a month long leave and a report date for Vietnam. And I was pretty much on the next plane out of Germany.

# 3

# THE LONG RIDE

SOMETIMES THE WORLD JUST RISES up and slaps you across the head.

That's what happened to me when I went to see the movie *Platoon*, directed brilliantly by Vietnam veteran Oliver Stone in the late 80's. In the opening sequence a guy is standing in front of the cargo door of what appears to be a C-17 Caribou, one of the ugliest things to ever fly. As I was starting to say to my wife that was the first thing I did in Vietnam, a graphic came on the screen saying September, 1967, the exact month of my arrival. It took me back in a big hurry.

The hours leading up to me arriving at that cargo door back in 1967 had been interesting. I left Seattle on a middle of the night flight to San Francisco. I said all my official goodbyes to my mom and sister and then my friends took me to the airport in a car so filled with marijuana smoke it was a miracle we could even breathe. This was their idea of an appropriate sendoff and who was I to argue?

Airlines had hearts in those days. It only took one glance at a gangly kid needing a haircut and wearing an ill-fitting dress uniform. They bumped me up to first class without a word. They didn't ask where I was headed. They knew. Please feel free to add a Dead Man Walking joke here or anywhere else on the pages to come. They just knew.

I got to my seat to find a skinny little guy already dozing against the window. He seemed to be dressed in some gauze like fabric. One look at me and he closed his eyes. He never said a word the whole flight. As we taxied out I recalled an argument at the ticket counter. It was about an expensive amplifier some guy didn't want to put in checked baggage. I took another look at my seat mate. Then it hit me. I believe I was sitting next to Donovan who had played a concert in Seattle earlier that night. My friends had made sure I was plenty stoned. I was scared and paranoid. I was on my way to Vietnam and now I seemed to be sitting next to the guy who sang "Mellow Yellow."

Right.

Dude. Wake up. Tell me the meaning of my bong-watered life. It seemed so highly significant in that moment. By the next morning I had to admit it didn't really mean a thing.

In those days soldiers didn't fly to Vietnam on military transports. About 150 of us flew from Travis Air Force base outside San Francisco on a Braniff 707. It was our last taste of civilization, our last one dollar mini-bottle and our last smile from a friendly flight attendant for what would prove to be a very long year. We learned that each and every one of those flight attendants had volunteered for the flights. Flying in and out of Vietnam was a little scarier than domestic routes. These women wouldn't have it any other way. Sure it was patriotic and all but mostly it was an act of the purest kindness. They knew what we were facing and they made those flights as jolly as possible. When we arrived we all got big smiles and pats on the shoulders. And almost every last one promised the impossible as we got off the plane. They said they would see us on the way back home.

By the way, Platoon won an Oscar for Best Picture and is still considered the best of the Vietnam movies. It was a great movie but to this day I would like someone to do a war movie about Vietnam with actors who were our age. We were children. We barely shaved. We were nineteen and twenty year-old draftees. Charlie Sheen was young in the movie but Tom Berenger and William Dafoe were well into their thirties. They looked like real soldiers. We didn't. We looked like kids dressed up for a high school play.

# 4

# BIEN HOA AIR BASE NEAR SAIGON

MY FIRST IN-COUNTRY VIETNAM EXPERIENCE is permanently stamped in my memory. I had been traveling in climate-controlled airliner comfort for probably sixteen hours. I stepped through the door of the plane and thought I had walked into a pizza oven. The heat was so intense I was literally gasping for air. The humidity swallowed me like a snake choking down a dead fat rodent. Never mind surviving a year of this. I thought I would pass out before I got down the steps to the tarmac. It really didn't seem like there was

any oxygen in this air. Nothing had even begun to prepare me for this. And as bad as it sounds, it never got any better. Like so many other things in the months to come, you just had to deal with it.

Bien Hoa was an assembly line for arriving soldiers. We all got new boots, new fatigues and a couple of canteens. In very short order, we found ourselves one at a time standing in front of a black sergeant who was going to tell us where we were headed.

Now here's a quick word about

The obligatory shot in front of the Charlie Company Death to the V.C. sign.

15

black army sergeants. In those days and maybe even now they essentially ran the army. These guys were smart. They had figured out there was very little discrimination among non-commissioned officers in the army. They did their jobs well. They got promoted and in some ways they created a fairly comfortable middle class life for themselves and their families inside the structured world of the military. For them it was a sharp contrast to what they might have experienced in civilian life.

So finally it was my turn. I stood in front of the sergeant. He took what seemed like an eternity to read over the papers he would soon be handing over to me. He seemed sympathetic and maybe even a little sad.

"Son," he said with what seemed to be genuine sorrow, "you are on your way to the Delta."

He then paused and shook his head a little and finished up in a gravelly, world weary voice. "Whole lotta bad shit goin' on down there."

Well, damn. That doesn't sound very good at all. I didn't know much about the geography of Vietnam but I knew from looking at the map that the Mekong River flowed in multiple branches south of Saigon. I could imagine rice patties. I would learn about mangrove swamps and tidal mud flats later. But for that moment I was much more concerned about the "bad shit goin' on down there." I had a gut sinking suspicion I was about to find out.

I would fly to my new basecamp with other replacement soldiers in that Caribou cargo plane I mentioned earlier. It was like a giant garbage dumpster with wings. Those wings were up high on fuselage and the engines looked better suited to garden machines than air travel. I had only flown at that point on commercial jets and I really was not too happy about having to fly on this crate. This sounds silly now but it just didn't look safe.

This became the first of many man-up moments in Vietnam. I talked to myself. You have got to prioritize your fears boy. It just doesn't make sense to be nervous about flying in a plane that is taking you to a place where actual people are going to try to kill you. I told myself to get on board. Don't worry about this plane. Worry about the fucking Viet Cong. That's the priority fear in this world. They're next and they really are dangerous.

*October 10, 1967*
*Dear Mom—*

*As you may have guessed your son is in Vietnam this week. And next, no doubt. It would be a big lie to say I liked it but it hasn't become totally unbearable yet. That comes next week.*

*Now for the cheerful part. My assignment is to the 9th INFANTRY DIVISION. I am presently at the Division Headquarters taking my 6 day indoctrination to jungle warfare.*

*I'm sure you'll be glad to hear that my battalion's base camp is located along the scenic Mekong River and our area of operations is known and loved by all as the Mekong Delta. That means rice paddies & jungles & Viet-Cong. Yech!*

*Anyway, I haven't been shot at yet so it could be worse.*

*I've managed to figure out the whole problem here. It's the South Vietnamese Army. They are Buddhists and they won't fight. Fortunately for our side, Christianity by way of Catholicism is taking over and teaching these poor passive savages the papal pleasures of killing a Commie for Christ.*

[Note: I had no idea what I was talking about at this point but I was always willing to express an opinion, even ignorant ones.]

*This whole war is run so ludicrously that it will take more time than I have now to describe it.*

*By the way, the Army messed up and gave me too much money. I sent $200 home to deposit. Also my bonds will begin November. Take care of my loot.*

[Note: You will notice throughout I am seemingly obsessed with my money. All I can say is that I entered the Army penniless and even a few hundred dollars seemed like a fortune to me in those days.]

*Tomorrow I go on my first jungle ambush patrol but it's just the final phase of the training program and amounts to nothing. Please write and let me know how you are.*

*Your Son #1,*
*Bill*

# 5

# WELCOME FNG'S

IN THE ARMY, THERE ARE labels for everything, formal and not so formal. We arrived formally at our unit as what the Army called Eleven Bravo Twenties (11B20). That was our Military Occupational Specialty. We were infantry privates. To everyone else we met we were called FNG's. That stood for Fucking New Guys. We were green, gullible and a dangerous liability to anyone standing nearby.

The photo below shows me, George Scott and Tom Maynard as total newbies. We all arrived at about the same time and quickly became fast friends. It just sort of made sense the new guys would bond. We were joining a veteran infantry outfit which had been through several recent horrific battles. The soldiers were all decent guys. They were helpful to a point. But they were way too weary to pay too much attention to replacement soldiers like us. We also figured out quickly we weren't normal replacements and this wasn't a normal Army unit. Our Charlie Company was part of one of the damnedest schemes the Army ever dreamed up and it made the notion of replacement troops much more personal.

Scott left, Lord and Maynard.

The 9th Infantry Division was an experiment. It was built from the ground up populated almost entirely with draftees who had been together from their first day in the Army. They did Basic Training together and then Advanced Infantry Training. They travelled to Vietnam together on a troop ship. They had been fighting together ever since. They were tight. Suffering serious casualties had made them tighter. This togetherness scheme might have seemed like a sound plan at some point but when the unit got to Vietnam someone woke up and realized that the entire division would be scheduled to go home on the same day. That had to be a monumental WTF moment for somebody. Getting them all here seemed okay but sending an entire infantry division home on the same day was idiotic and impossible.

Here's how it generally worked. In most outfits soldiers came and went on their one year tours and there was a constant flux. Replacement soldiers tended to fill in for the guys who went home. In Charlie Company nobody had rotated "back to the World" as they had in other units. They were only eight months into their tours. So as replacements we didn't come in to take the place of some lucky guy who was back at home bragging about his sexual conquests. We were there to replace long time good friends who had been killed in combat or wounded so badly they couldn't return. So while we were treated well, we weren't on the original team. We would never be on the original team. There were even some skeptics who were understandably a little standoffish. We were living reminders of dead friends.

So Scott, Maynard and I learned a lot on our own as we went along. We endured yet another label for guys like us. Cherry. What's a Cherry in this context? It's an infantry soldier who has not yet been under enemy fire. Nobody really wanted to be a

Cherry but we weren't hot to lose that Cherry either. We didn't exactly want to go out and get shot at. The idea of being shot at had very limited appeal. So this was just one of many amusing little Vietnam paradoxes you laughed off before you went nuts.

Charlie Company was about a hundred and twenty-five guys and was part of a much larger military group called the Mobile Riverine Force. We traveled the rivers of South Vietnam on flat bottomed landing craft that dropped us into rural areas where we were expected to chase down Viet Cong. Some days it was the boats. Some days it was helicopters. But the result was always the same. We were in wet, muddy rice paddies, swamps and small strips of jungle. The learning curve was steep. As a student, I was a little slow.

Within just a few seconds of stepping off the landing craft the first time I realized that this was a bad place to carry your wallet in your back pocket. Mine was as soaked as it had been when I was pushed into a

Tango Boats, our main method of transport provided by what we called the Brown Water Navy.

swimming pool in high school. I must have sworn and complained because the guy next to me held up his wallet in a perfectly neat plastic bag. This was 1967. We had not yet landed on the moon. And I had never before seen a zip lock bag.

"Available at the PX," my fellow soldier said.

Five minutes later we walked through a chest deep canal in banana grove. I was gazing at my first ever banana trees and imagining Viet Cong behind every one when I realized that my shirt pocket was a bad place to carry my cigarettes. Now they were soaked. I bitched again. The same guy showed me a hard plastic case the size of a cigarette package. It slipped neatly under the elastic band on his helmet. Apparently the helmet was safe. If you got your helmet under water you were a real fuck up. I was learning all this much to my colleague's amusement.

"Also available at the PX," he said with a big smile.

There were plenty of other lessons along the way. How do you remove the first leech that attaches itself to you? Squirt liquid mosquito repellant on the head. How do you cook C-Rations in the can? Light a small chunk of C-4 plastic explosive on fire, of course. The first time you put a match to plastic explosive can be little nerve-wracking but boy did that shit burn hot and cook fast. Finally, what do you do when you're riding a helicopter into a landing zone and someone is shooting at you? Jump! They're not shooting at you they're shooting at the helicopter.

Along the way, Scott Maynard and I lost our Cherry status and slowly came of age in this alternate universe we now inhabited. We talked all the time and shared the stories of our lives. If we had been college roommates we would have stayed in touch forever. Somehow after Vietnam, we never spoke again. We were extremely tight buddies. We lived through huge hardships together. But when it ended we all left at different times and went our separate ways. I can only speak for myself but this was the first stage of what would become a lifetime of general denial. There were quite a few guys I cared about a great deal. I have thought about them often over the years. We laughed together, fought together and grieved together. But when I left I vowed I would only look forward. All my life I have looked forward. In many ways I'm convinced that's the best outlook you can have on living. But it came with a price. I walled off my worst experiences but at the same time walled off some of the best people I met along the way.

*October 30, 1969*

*Dear Mom —*

*How's things? I really have no news of importance other than I am alive and quite sound after my first month here which in itself should surprise no one. I can't really say that the pressure is off but after being out a few times I have a lot more confidence in myself and it really isn't so scary after all. When you get out on an operation they run you kind of hard and you're too tired to think about being scared and when something does happen, which isn't too regular, it all happens so fast that there isn't time to worry about it.*

*Hubert Humphrey, let's see, I think he is the mayor of Minneapolis, was here the other day and we got called out to secure the bay when he landed.*

[Note: Here's where I started fudging a bit with my mom on what we were really doing on what were called Search and Destroy missions. I'm kind of doing the same things as I write for you readers. I think she and most of you can imagine a lot. And I did know that Humphrey was the Vice-President by then. He had inconvenienced me the year before in Berlin when we had to put on riot gear to repel imaginary protestors. And oddly enough I actually got to know him some years later as a grad student in D.C. He would stay late at any news conference and talk with our small group of student reporters who were by then in awe of him.]

*All we did was go out and secure the water around the assault boats safely out of sight. I guess that is the general thing to do when the big wigs come over here. Show them the fine living and working conditions and the clean mess halls of the Remington Rangers (clerks) in Saigon and hide the infantry so no one gets the picture of just exactly what we go through. I'd like to see old Bob McNamera tramping through the rice paddies with me someday.*

*I don't know if I'm changing my opinion about the war itself or not but I've learned a lot more about it. The S. Vietnamese don't really appreciate the help they get, they just use old Uncle Sam to get the Yankee Dollar just like everybody else in the world.*

*Their Army, called ARVN's (Army of the Republic of Vietnam and pronounced Arvan) is the sorriest mess I have ever seen and now after the latest elections they plan to use the American Forces for all fighting and use the ARVN's for "civil affairs" whatever that means.*

*I do know that if they get in trouble we have to go in and bail them out and if they see an American unit getting beat they'll sit there 200 yards away and watch without lifting a finger. So we aren't really assisting anyone we are outrightly doing it for them and they are quite content to let us since it also benefits their economy.*

*I guess we haven't any choice but I personally care very little for the Vietnamese people and I certainly don't feel that I am doing them any favors nor will I go out of my way to do them any favors. Turn it around and the average civilian would slit a G.I.'s throat for a can of C-Ration Ham and Lima Beans.*

*Sorry if I don't sound the cheerful lad I usually do but if I didn't complain there wouldn't be much to write about.*

*Again, I plead, send books. True magazine and Superman comics are getting rather dull.*

*Take it easy and be sure and write.*

*Love,*
*Bill, your #1 Son*

# 6

# THE LISTENING POST

A COUPLE OF DAYS AFTER I learned how to keep my smokes out of the swamp I had yet another of those man up moments. We were setting up a perimeter for the night in a typical rice paddy setting. We tended to set up next to the bamboo and grass hootches dotting the landscape. They were on dry ground and their owners vanished as soon as we came along.

I wasn't a radio guy yet. I was still a brand new rifleman. I was unsure of myself and very nervous about my surroundings. Can a Cherry be green? Yes he can.

My squad leader at the time pointed to two of us and said something like, "when it gets dark I want the two of you to take a radio out there about a hundred yards to that second dike and set up a listening post." What he meant was to go out there and spend the entire night waiting to see if someone attacked us.

He was very matter of fact about it like this happened all the time so I did not say all the things flying through my head at that moment.

A weary me on an unknown date in Vietnam.

"Are you fucking nuts? I just got here. Are you trying to kill me in my first week?" I did not say anything.

But what was he thinking? I was clueless. The listening post was going to be there as an early warning if the Viet Cong were going to attack our positions at night. We were essentially expendable for the safety of the larger group. I just didn't think I would be deemed expendable quite this soon.

It got dark and we waded out to the second dike. We split the watch into two-hour segments. We clicked our radio handset every hour on the hour to let everyone know we were all right. I think that was the night I learned the term sitrep meant situation report. We weren't allowed to actually talk. We just clicked if we were okay.

I was up all night nervous about everything. My partner was less nervous. Jesus, he snored. I kept waking him up until finally at about five am he rolled down behind the dike and was fumbling around mysteriously when I realized he was lighting a cigarette. We're in pitch darkness alone in the middle of Viet Cong territory. We're already a juicy target. His match was like a flare going off identifying our position despite his weary worded claim nobody could see it. I was not convinced.

Somehow, we survived the night and life went on. But I was always just a little curious how a Cherry boy like me had been chosen for this role so soon after my arrival. It just seemed odd.

When I finally got my answer I learned it was a decision the squad leader had come to with a considerable amount of soul searching. Only I had to wait a little more than forty five years to find out what he was thinking.

*November 8, 1967*

*Dear Mom —*

*Well we just got back from another unimportant and not too interesting operation. This time we used assault boats and helicopters. The helicopters were fun to ride but you can get to feeling insecure in a big hurry if you hear funny crackling noises.*

*We set up in a V.C. village one night and one of the squads was set up in a hootch where some old Vietnamese lady was having a baby. You should have seen them in the morning. We got a couple of rather frantic calls on the radio about the whole thing and it was rather amusing. Anyway she had a nice young Viet Cong girl.*

*I am so sick of C-Rations I could throw up. I have a good plan for packages however. Send stuff like pre-sweetened Kool-Aid (you were right) and canned chili and meat balls and stuff like that. Anything that comes in a small can that would be good. They have to be small enough to stuff in a wool sock though because that's how I carry food when out in the muck and they have to be cans because they get wet about twenty times a day before I can get a chance to eat. Believe me anything is better than Ham and Lima Beans. Also I like Niblets Corn. Just anything that looks good and comes in a small can.*

*I can't begin to tell you how frustrating it is to try and keep cigarettes dry here. The only way is to keep them up inside your steel helmet 'cause that's the only dry part of you. The other day I got into some red ants and started slapping at them on my neck and I knocked my helmet into the rice paddy. Needless to say after fishing it out of 2 or 3 feet of mud and water the cigarettes, matches, book and cocoa stored up there were all destroyed. Also, needless to say I cursed vehemently.*

*I got a letter from you yesterday asking to write more and I'll try to do better but they do keep me busy.*

*Take it easy and don't worry. Only ten months left. Less than that now.*

*Your son,*
*Swamp Rat*

*P.S. I also want a record album called "Fire" by the "Doors". If you can, send it and take it out of my money.*

*PPSS Also I need film for a Kodak 104 Instamatic. The film is type CX 126-20 or else 126 cartridge.*

# 7

# WHAT WE HAVE HERE IS A FAILURE TO COMMUNICATE

YOU READ THE LETTER HOME of me asking for canned food to supplement my diet. It seemed pretty simple, right? It wasn't.

Let's think about this. It's sort of like a high school math question. How many calories would a 170lb man burn carrying say fifty pounds of radio, batteries, weapons, ammo, poncho, water, maps, food, snacks, books and a few scraps of paper to write letters home? Let's say he hikes for twelve hours in 100 degree heat through slippery mud caked rice paddies, swamps and other malarial water bodies of all types. I will modestly guess two or three shit tons. We burned through calories at about the same rate a flame thrower could burn through grass hootches.

Many times after a day like this a helicopter would drop by with a few cases of C-Rations and some large cans of potable water. The helicopter then skedaddled back to some place with a nice kitchen. I promise they never stayed for supper.

So now it was time for your daily surprise. In each box of

A hungry me eating what appears to be a freshly liberated banana.

C-Rations you would get a baby sized Hershey bar, then a dessert which was a tiny can of fruit or pound cake, and a "main course" to use a term that would have surely mystified the employees back in the C-Rations kitchens. This main course came in a can about as tall but much skinnier than a can of beans. If you were really lucky you might get the spaghetti and meatballs. Heat that up with plastic explosives and you at least get something that tastes good. It's wasn't enough, but it was tasty.

There were several other less tasty options and then there was the ugliest stepsister in the entire canned food universe. Ham and Lima Beans. Remember, we were kids, right. No kid ever ate lima beans where I came from. And these weren't just lima beans. You opened the can and stared at a vomit glaze of green slimy nuggets encased in a congealed white lardy fat substance. Not improving the color pallet at all were the tiny chunks of pig meat that must have started life as a wild boar hog rambling though the bushes of East Texas. The meat had pinkish tones but with enough obvious gristle you could be sure to get a good workout session for the old molars. It was probably what we served to prisoners before someone discovered water boarding.

It was so bad I couldn't even trade it to a ten year old for a bottle of coke in a local village one day.

"You bad, G.I.," the kid said with a sneer. He followed that with the pinnacle of Far East insults.

"You numba ten."

Jesus. I was just thirsty. Who knew this fucking kid could read?

I am providing you all this background so you will be able to truly appreciate how hungry I was and the absurdity of the comedy that followed. It sort of starts with, "Dear mom, I'm starving. Don't send cookies, send food."

If your kid is half a world away and asks for something, most moms answer the call very quickly. My mom went above and beyond. She didn't just go to Safeway like I asked to buy canned chili, corn beef hash or Spaghetti O's. That wasn't good enough for her kid. She went to the specialty food counter at a downtown department store. She bought the most unbelievable shit I could have ever imagined.

I was overjoyed when the package arrived. Finally, food I could carry out in the bush and not starve. And then I opened the box. There before me were about a dozen little flat cans of fancy seafood products. Remember those flat cans with the long key that let you peel back the lid. Those were the ones. Fancy sardines from Spain. Smoked oysters from Norway or someplace. Olives in oil. Cheeses. Clams. And a bunch of stuff I couldn't readily identify.

Now let's review the circumstances. I live in a world of dirt and mud. From time to time people shoot at us. We don't wash our hands. We don't eat off plates. If I sit down to eat I am sitting on the ground. I am half-starved. I would be delirious at the vision of a can of Chef Boyardee Beefaroni. Remember those great ads. Kids all over the world singing "Hooray for Beefaroni!"

Instead I will sit down in the mud and crack open a lovely tin of clams. And be careful not to tip that tiny tin because everything is packed in olive oil. You wouldn't want that to spill and run together with the many layers of brown swamp crap already adorning your battle fatigues. And here's best part. This stuff didn't just taste bad, it wasn't just messy, it was also vastly more expensive than the stuff I actually wanted.

You will see I noted this politely in my next letter home. I don't think I ever really changed her mind about fancy food but she did adjust. I didn't save any of the letters my mom wrote back to me but she did have a pretty good sense of humor. She apologized for our little failure to communicate but she couldn't quite let go of the fine quality goods she had sent. As I recall she may have even slyly implied that I wasn't that sharp, classy son she had hoped for after I told her I hated that food.

Mail took forever in those days. Packages were even slower. In the end, I got my requested canned goods and the clock slowly ticked away toward that flight home.

*November 12, 1967*
*Dear Mom —*
*Well, I got your package just before our last operation and it was very nice. One thing, Mom, I don't think you quite realize the situation. It's not that I don't like Smoked Baby Oysters imported from Norway or whatever but a can of Chili would be far more practical. Contrary to popular opinion this is not a picnic or a nature hike with the National Audubon Society. I really looked rather incongruous sitting on a stump in a mangrove swamp eating Smoked Baby Oysters with my C-Ration spoon.*

*I appreciate the effort Mom but I really don't demand all these imported specialties. I think perhaps you should forsake Frederick & Nelson for your local A & P.*

*I also got a coffee can full of fruit cake and marshmallows from the McLeods which is rather embarrassing since I haven't written them yet. They must have got my address from John.*

[John McLeod was a friend from all the way back in elementary school. I had lived with his family during the last few months of high school. He was at the Naval Academy while I was in Vietnam. We have remained friends our whole lives.]

*Dad and Sally's birthdays are within a week and they got together and gave each other a color TV which is rather extravagant since they watch very little TV anyway.*

[Note: My parents divorced when I was 11 or 12. My dad had remarried and moved to Boston with his new wife who was very nice to my sister and me. And perhaps a little out of character, my mom did not seem hostile to this new person in our lives.]

*This last 3 day weekend we went out on helicopters and stomped around in some of the worst terrain I've ever seen. It was a large patch of jungle that has grown near the Delta rice paddies and you can barely get through the growth and about every twenty meters there is a small canal with the foulest leech-filled water I've ever seen about shoulder deep. To make two or three miles in a day is quite an accomplishment.*

*My feet are totally unrecognizable after this and have been raw and red all over. I think it's one of these deals that is bad enough to be uncomfortable but not bad enough to get out of any field duty.*

*I really haven't any real news because there isn't much to tell about. I'm still all healthy and intent on staying so. Time is going fairly rapidly and it seems hard to believe I've been here nearly a month and a half. I hope the rest goes by as quickly.*

*I still need books and I'm even considering taking a look into correspondence courses. In between operations I have usually two or three days in which to prepare for the next operation and I'm sure I'd have enough time to take some sort of flunkly class.*

*Well, the mail is here and I hope I get some letters. I'll write again soon.*

*Your son,*
*Von Zipper*

[Note: I am telling my mom about a lot of the peripheral stuff like logistics and sore feet while not revealing perhaps the most important thing. We were scared. At this point we had been subjected to casualties from booby traps and short ambushes. Honestly, that was expected and routine. What haunted us was what the older guys had survived before I arrived which was something we still believed could happen at any time.]

# 8

# JUNE 19, 1967

VIETNAM HAD A WAY OF dealing out fear on multiple levels. Early on I was seriously affected by the older guys' descriptions of a battle on June 19, 1967, which took place several months before I arrived. By older guys I mean they had been there eight months longer than I had. Many of them had a haunted look. At first I thought all the "older" Vietnam soldiers were that way. I was wrong.

These guys were haunted by surviving the living hell of being caught out in an open rice paddy where they had been ambushed by a much larger Viet Cong force. The V.C. were dug into protected bunkers. Some of the lucky Charlie Company soldiers were able to get behind small dikes in the paddies. Most had nowhere to hide. Eleven Charlie Company soldiers were killed, most within the first few minutes. Dozens more were wounded. Many of the survivors who had no place to hide were forced to play dead.

When these guys talked about June 19th they spoke with a faraway gaze. And it was never June 19th. It was June THE 19th. The scene was blazoned in their minds then and probably still is now. I will spare you many of the heartbreaking minute by minute details of this day but they are well

Soldiers dangerously bunched up in an open rice paddy.

told in Andrew Wiest's book *The Boys of '67*. He reported many chilling personal accounts of an entire day of seemingly unmitigated hell on earth. Fear, pain, death and heroism all had their moments before it was over.

The battle didn't really turn until the tide came in and the stream levels rose. A Navy gunboat was able to get upstream close enough to help. By all accounts our Company Commander, Captain Herbert Lind, took a radio out into the most dangerous area of the battle and directed the gunboat fire on to the bunkers which were ultimately destroyed. That led to follow up counter attacks that eventually resulted in huge losses for the Viet Cong.

American losses were huge as well. Beyond those in our Charlie Company, Alpha Company in our battalion had it even worse. Twenty-seven soldiers killed and scores more wounded. By the end of the day it effectively did not exist as a military unit. Almost everyone was a casualty. One soldier letter home reported that only twelve men out of 134 in Alpha Company were not killed or wounded. He said the battle lasted 23 hours and "it was the most violent, frightening, exhausting and ugly thing I will ever see."

I was scared mostly because I thought this was my future. I could easily imagine this nightmarish scenario played out over and over during the next year. The odds of survival at that early point looked pretty bleak.

I didn't realize it at the time but June 19, 1967 was a tipping point in the Vietnam War in two significant ways. First, it changed the way both sides did battle in the Delta. And second, in a much larger sense it helped boost the emerging anti-war sentiments back in the states.

In the Delta, never again did 9th Division soldiers allow themselves to get bunched up in the open like they did that day. I'm sure there must have been lead patrol or "point" units that day but going forward in time those small lead units were much farther out in front to disrupt any potential ambush before it could result in so many casualties.

Andrew Wiest quotes an after action report by company commander Herbert Lind who wrote two clear warnings to the staff of the entire brigade.

First:

*(The enemy) will keep track of your movements and positions. Positioning for a night stand should not be accomplished until after dark.*

And second, in a not so thinly veiled reference to the clustering up of soldiers in an open area that led to so many casualties on June 19th:

*Never cross an open area with the main body until the recon elements have thoroughly searched areas of cover ahead. Keep point elements at three men or less. In some areas they will need to precede the main body by 1,000 meters. Never pull them in less than 500 meters in rice paddy areas.*

On June 19th, the main body of soldiers was in some cases less than 50 meters from the enemy when the ambush began.

It was also a tactical lesson for the Viet Cong, though. Their ambush was successful only up to a point. By the time it was over the V.C. had lost hundreds of men even if you discount for the often inflated body county figures reported in Vietnam. Their unit was all but wiped out. It proved to the V.C. that they could not take and hold territory because eventually superior American firepower would locate and destroy them. That's what ultimately happened on June 19, 1967. By trying to hold on to territory they were killed. V.C. ambushes would continue throughout the remainder of the war but in the Delta they became quick hit and run ambushes that generally lasted only a few minutes before the V.C. vanished back into the landscape. No military unit could survive taking the level of casualties the Viet Cong took in the June 19th battle.

The changing tactics on both sides resulted in far fewer casualties for both sides after this battle. Charlie Company casualties after this time were significantly reduced. In fact, I believe we had more casualties from booby traps than direct enemy fire after June 19th.

Back home in America things were changing as well.

The Battle of June 19th triggered immediate reactions. Public opinion at home trumped whatever happened on the battlefield. This is the Los Angeles Times front page three days after the battle.

This was Alpha Company. The headline is alarmist but not inaccurate. It simply goes straight to the heart of an issue we all lived with. Everything about Vietnam was a matter of perspective.

Soldier holds up *L.A.Times* article about Alpha Company. Many soldiers considered this one-sided in that it didn't depict the bigger picture of what had happened.

Forget about who won the battle. In the end Vietnam battles were like that. Winning on the battlefield was nothing compared to the shock value of this article. My friends in Charlie Company believe to this day they fought hard and won that battle. Our CO risked his life to ensure the Viet Cong paid the price for their audacious action. But nobody back home cared about military victories. Nobody back home looked for a V.C. body count headline. Instead they were traumatized beyond all measure that this many Americans could be killed and wounded in a single action.

The country just wasn't ready to think about that many American casualties. At the time we weren't really that far removed from just having "advisors" in Vietnam. The big troop build-up was still in progress. This was one of the first mass casualty results and it didn't play well at home at all. Ironically, the American people wanted soldiers to be safe and at the same time they were pulling the rug out from under the military missions we had been given.

I think many attitudes started changing with this event and eight months later when Viet Cong sappers (explosive experts) attacked the U.S. Embassy in Saigon in front of network news cameras during the Tet Offensive the majority of the American people were already shifting to an anti-war stance. And with that shift Americans began to look down on the soldiers themselves for our continued military actions in Vietnam.

It didn't take much time for the discontent back home to be felt on the front lines of increasingly irrelevant battles. This was a holy shit moment for a great many of us. I repeatedly use the term "nothing to win" because there were two conflicts. One was in Vietnam and one was at home. One was military, one was political. One was fought in the rice paddies and the jungles. One was fought in the streets and in the halls of power. There were endless shades of gray about right or wrong. This was a country that had been totally united behind World War II. It was now paralyzed by angry, outspoken critics and inflexible leaders. Vietnam flipped the country upside down and it took forever to sort it all out.

In the end, as a country, we were stupid and indecisive. We employed half measure tactics in Vietnam. Imbecilic pride delayed any political decisions at home. And here's what happened. We waffled away eight more years and well beyond thirty thousand more American lives before we could bring it all to an end. And that's unconscionable. At the same time, when all was said and done, America turned its back on our youngest ever generation of soldiers who had already suffered enough on the battlefield. I can't stress enough how young we were. Imagine the psychological cross currents youthful soldiers faced terrorized by combat and then often repudiated as monsters when they finally got "safely" home.

Lucky ones like me were able to compartmentalize, wall it off and look forward. That wasn't possible for potentially millions of others. Their lives got stuck in the confusion and the bitterness that resulted from these whipsaw forces affecting them. How many good people led angry, unfulfilled lives? How many were unable to finish school or find good jobs? How many turned to drugs and alcohol? How many turned to suicide? Frankly, how many are homeless in our streets right now five decades removed from all this?

It would be so satisfying to hold someone accountable for all this. I'd love to blame someone. But the more I think about this I can't find the bad guy. I can't name that one group who did this. We were all victims of historical forces beyond our control and I think we are all struggling now to make amends. In that sense, it is never too late to honor those who served.

# 9

# VERMIN AND INDIGNITIES TO MY PERSON

THERE WERE SO MANY SOURCES of discomfort in Vietnam beyond the war itself. People always ask, "what was it like?" Sometimes I was unable to avoid this question so I worked up a few stock answers. They are all true and in a way told their own story. I tended to start with the red ants. Why red ants? Simple. They are the most insidious, vicious little six-legged vermin bastards on the face of the earth. In Vietnam they didn't just bite, they attacked. They seemed to attack for the sheer joy of it. They climbed up off the ground, they jumped out of trees, they got under your clothes and like tiny rabid pit bulls they sank their jaws into your skin and refused to let go. Walk through the bush, sit down to rest or lie down to sleep. Plan to be nipped.

Does it hurt? Holy shit, yes. They are said to be descended from wasps. The bite feels like a modest bee sting. And even when you pull them off or smash them to a nasty rust-colored slime, the bite keeps hurting for several minutes. They were everywhere and they attacked in numbers. There are plenty of stories, perhaps a little exaggerated, of soldiers standing up in the middle of battles and tearing off their shirts to rid themselves of red ants. They were a relentless enemy and they attacked us a helluva lot more often than the Viet Cong. They were among the countless indignities I was clearly not prepared for by growing up in a quiet Seattle suburb.

There were also death dealing bees, squadrons of mosquitos and all manner of gross things you never imagined would happen to you.

I'm sorry. Did I fail to mention leeches? Leeches were yet another daily inconvenience. They lived in all the streams, canals and rice paddies we waded through. I don't know how they survived without infantry soldiers to suck on but

Leeches are sneaky. You never felt one until it had had its fill.

they made a heck of a good living at our expense. They start out as vile little inch-long, gray-green slimy worm-looking things. They could expand to three or more inches long once they attached themselves to us and started sucking our blood. You couldn't feel them but every now and then we had to stop, drop our trousers and inspect ourselves. They were often all over our legs. How they got there is still a bit of a mystery to me. We tucked our pant legs into our boots. We cinched our belts up tightly. Still, they managed to get to our legs and have a good gorge. If you shot enough army bug repellant on their heads they would drop off but you didn't want to smash them because it was kind of icky to see your own blood pouring out of them.

The scary and possibly apocryphal story about leeches is the one about the soldier who had one crawl inside the hole in his penis. The leech head was literally inside him and bug spray did nothing to help. The story went that he had to be choppered back to base camp to have it surgically removed. I don't know if it was true but it packed a lot of cringe worthy credibility back then.

And then the real scary stuff. Snakes.

Snakes? Sure. There were plenty of poisonous snakes although we really didn't all see that many of them. We did worry about them quite a bit. We were terrified of something called a bamboo viper. Without the benefit of the Internet in those days to check the facts we tended to believe the stories of how a bamboo viper could kill you in just a matter of seconds.

Some of our jolly old time sergeants told us if one of them bites your finger you won't have time to cut off your hand. You'd be dead first. It didn't help matters that they started a rumor at our basecamp in Dong Tam that a

The Bamboo Viper (peterallanlloyd.com).

bamboo viper was found in a shit can under one of the outhouses on the base. That meant you couldn't even relax to go to the bathroom. Trust me, we always took a good long look at the bucket we were about to sit over. It was a standard involuntary inspection. Those bastard sergeants knew exactly what they were doing when they told us this. They were screwing with our already messed up heads. And it worked.

And while the Internet now tells me a bamboo viper couldn't really kill someone in just seconds you better get some anti-venom fast if you get bitten by one of those suckers. Without it you've got an hour tops before you stop breathing.

Now my favorite snake story is real up close and personal. One of the things we did on a regular basis was check out and search "hootches." They were the bamboo and grass huts that housed much of the rice farming population in the Delta. They were all very similar. There was a slab of mahogany that served as a bed. There was bin that held recently harvested rice. And there was a mud bunker that families generally used to protect themselves from shelling or bombing. We would go in pointing our eyes and our weapons at the bunker since if there was any danger it would come from there. I did that one day only to look up and find myself literally eyeball to eyeball with about a twelve foot long jungle python sliding along the bamboo rafters.

I swear his head must have been the size of my fist and that head was literally two feet from my nose. Maybe it just felt like my heart stopped. I froze. His tongue waggled at me. I blinked. He didn't. I slowly backed up. Finally, when my brain kicked back online a few seconds later things became a little clearer to me. This menacing, huge shithead serpent was somebody's pet. I'm sure he kept the place rodent free. Maybe they even snuggled with him at night. All I know is that he scared the bejesus out of me that day and I never forgot it.

And one more thing, I hate to admit this but even today, eons after the probably phony story was told, I still take a look inside every toilet bowl before I sit down.

*November 15, 1967*
*Dear Mom—*

*I don't know why I am writing since I'm totally angered by everyone I know since I have heard from no one for 3 whole days now.*

[Note: Just kidding. This happened all the time.]

*Remember the Dear Abby clipping you sent me? It came out in the Stars & Stripes today. You should have heard the guffaws. Do the whole U.S. Army a favor and disregard Abigail. All I want, and desperately at that, is a couple of small cans of chili and some reading matter. In addition to stock old novels I would like books on the Hindu Religion. I'm curious about Eastern religions in general.*

[Note: The Dear Abby column I scoffed at was about a letter from a soldier named Sgt. Billy Thompson. He wrote to her saying all he wanted for Christmas was a letter from home. Sounds pretty lame, right? Well, it seemed lame to me and my friends. I was wrong. Completely wrong as it turns out. Abby put her foot to the metal. This letter and her response spawned something called Operation Dear Abby. The result was Americans sent hundreds of thousands of letters to soldiers overseas and kept sending them right up until 9/11. That was when Anthrax fears about mail moved the whole thing online where it got millions of hits. So, note to young Bill from old Bill: Abigail wins this round. You blew this one big time.]

*I am enclosing a picture of Baby Huey and his boys.* [Hubert Humphrey] *Remember I told you he was here. It was taken on the USS Benewah which is one of our three MRF* [Mobile Riverine Force] *troop ships. I stay on the USS Westchester County. I am also enclosing some of the propaganda we pass out to civilians on operations. This particular piece tells them how much the U.S. will pay for the different weapons used here. The only thing I wonder is just how many people in the Mekong Delta can read? Oh Well.*

*When are you going to buy a new car? I've got to have something to operate with when I get back because I won't have a very nice car myself. I consider the money I save in the place as blood money and I'm not going to squander it.*

*Brainstorm!! If you want a picture or two of your boy at the war, send film for my camera. Type 126-20 Kodacolor Prints. I get them developed by sending them to Hawaii and I get a roll of film back with the prints but it takes some time to get the ball rolling.*

*How's winter coming? Or is it? Before it's over you may appreciate apartments a lot more. It's hot here and only rains when I'm on an operation and when it does rain, well, they call them monsoons and I call them oceans. You wouldn't believe it.*

*Just think, I'll be home in 9 ¾ months. Isn't that a nice thing to look forward to?*

*I got a new and better job by the way. I carried a radio for one day and did so well they made me the platoon leader radio man. It has very few good points and a great deal of bad. In addition to packing that thing everyplace the Lt. wants to go (and they do run all over, sort of like a chicken who has just been disjointed at the neck), I am told that snipers fully approve of radio men as targets.*

*I think I'll go back to just being a stock old line doggie because it's kind of a pain in the neck to have to follow somebody around. Besides I have to carry the gun and everything else anyway.*

[Note: I never was able to ditch the radio. Once I carried the radio it was mine. Within a month I had been bumped up to carry the Company Commander's radio. In the end, it was a good move for me because I was engaged and very much in the know about what was going on. I don't know if that was any strategic benefit to anyone but I certainly liked knowing what was going on.]

*Well, I'll sign off now but you'll probably be hearing from me.*

*Your humble son,*
*Alfred E. Neuman*

# 10

# SCOTTIE AND THE STICK

ONE ENDURING MEMORY OF THE Vietnam War for me was seeing George Scott pounding his way through a minefield with a giant stick. He would slam the stick into the spot he planned to put his next step. The theory was if something blew up it would hurt you a lot less from three feet away than if you were stepping directly on it. Scott was a hard-scrapple, dutiful Oklahoman who did his job. Devising a way to make it slightly less hazardous was somewhere between wildly practical and pure genius. As the time went on that day we passed that stick to pretty much everyone in the squad and somehow we all got out safely.

Scott was our champion in that minefield. He had made beating the minefield a team sport. Of all the crap we did over there I think we may have felt more camaraderie that day more than any other. We all shouldered the burden, played the stick game and got through it. It may sound dumb now but there was a lot of back-slapping at the end of that day. But no high fives. High fives did not enter American culture for another decade.

I'll take a rough guess and say we lost more than a dozen guys to

Tu Dia might mean "your day" in Spanish but it meant booby traps in Vietnamese.

booby traps in Charlie Company during my time there. Not lost as in killed. Lost as in injured to the point they were sent to the hospital in Japan or sent home. That doesn't sound like a huge number but when you consider we put a hundred or so people in the field on any given mission it's a pretty decent percentage. It was certainly a cause for considerable concern for those of us out there in the bush.

I'll just come right out and say this. The Army was box of rocks stupid when it came to booby traps. The Vietnamese marked most of the booby trap areas to protect their own people. There were little signs that said Tu Dia. I have seen various translations of that but the most obvious was "death zone." The Army must have believed the Viet Cong were hiding things near these signs so the brass insisted guys like us should walk through the areas and check them out.

Our perspective was a little different. Sure they may be hiding something. That's why God invented the B-52 which can put a 500lb bomb on a mail box from 50,000 feet above. Whatever was hidden would turn to dust and grunts like us would still have all their toes at the end of the day. Sounds simple, right? As it turns out we did not run the Army.

We were spared some of the nastiest booby traps in the Delta because it was too wet to dig holes for the infamous punji sticks and all the variations. I only saw one punji pit the whole time I was there. What we generally faced were explosive booby traps. The Claymore mine was an insidious American product that was generally set off by a person hiding in the bushes. It was a semi-circle of plastic explosive shaped to spray ball bearings over a wide area. Then there was the Bouncing Betty. If you stepped on this it popped up and blew you to bits about waist high. It was rare but deadly. In our case it was mostly the notorious Toe-Popper making our lives stressful.

Now I hated the Viet Cong for all the obvious reasons. But they were smart and clever. They had figured out that killing a soldier didn't drain our resources anywhere near as much as a good, serious wounding. If you kill someone they get zipped in a bag and sent home. If you wound them you tie up medics to treat them, choppers to dust them off, hospitals to rehab them often for months at a time and so on. Someone estimated that it took nine times the resources to treat a wounded soldier than it took to send a dead soldier home. I have no source for that figure but it sounds right.

So, the Toe Popper.

It was so dastardly simple. A .50 caliber shell casing filled with plastic explosive and set off with a tiny pressure detonator. It couldn't have cost a dollar for the Viet Cong to make. The morning Scottie grabbed the stick, and one of the reasons he was being so careful, one of our guys had already stepped on a Toe Popper. I was close by and had seen the boot blown off his foot and the mangled, burned mess it left behind. I can still hear his cursing before the morphine took hold. It was painful and frightening. But even then you could tell he would survive and probably not even lose the foot. But there would be hospitals, surgeries and months of rehab in his immediate future. That's exactly what the Viet Cong wanted.

Scottie's stick was a low tech counter-measure to the Toe Popper. We all congratulated him for his wily ways which produced his usual unassuming, "Aw Shucks" sort of response. He was a team player who never sought the spotlight. Ironically, Scottie beat the Toe Poppers that day only to fall victim to a Claymore mine a couple of months later. He was on a night patrol near our base camp at Dong Tam when the mine was detonated. We were all in close enough proximity to hear the explosion and follow the radio chatter. Scottie and several others had been wounded. He had apparently been hit by more than a dozen ball bearings along one arm and shoulder. He was not in great shape but it was clearly a survivable wound.

But here's the final stinging upshot of all this and I think it affected a lot of Vietnam friendships. By the time we got back to basecamp he was gone. He was sent to Japan or somewhere. His gear stowed away. His bunk was open for the next guy.

This was goodbye Vietnam style. Scott was a true friend I slogged through the shit with for many long months. Remember, we were FNG's together. And then boom. He's hit. He's gone. We never speak again. I could have and should have tracked him down. I'm sure I planned that I would track him down. He probably thought the same. But then life intervenes, the denial starts, the compartmentalization, the forget the past and only look forward mentality and pretty soon fifty years have gone by.

I have thought about Scottie many times. He's another one I hope has led a long and happy life. He earned it.

# 11

# SNIPERS

WRITING DOWN ALL MY THOUGHTS on Vietnam has one huge plus. I can go on a rant and there's really nobody to stop me.

A year or two back a friend at work asked casually if I had seen the movie "American Sniper."

"No," I replied. "I would never go to a movie that glorified a sniper, American or otherwise."

He was shocked. He had a close relative in the Marines. He reminded me that the central character in this movie was American, an Iraq war hero. He suggested I should be able to know the difference between a good sniper and a bad sniper.

My reply had nothing to do with rational thought.

"There is no difference between a good sniper and bad sniper," I said. "They're all still snipers. They sit back in a concealed nest and kill people from sometimes as much as a mile away. To me it's a job for only the most ruthless among us."

That went over poorly then and it might come across poorly now to you. It is however, exactly what I feel. Remember, I was the guy sporting a tall whip antenna most of my time in Vietnam. The Viet Cong would rather have shot officers but officers never wore any obvious insignia of rank. That made radio guys like me an obvious and easily targeted second choice.

Now you can convince me snipers may be a cruel necessity of war but you can't stop me from recoiling at the thought of them in the way most people react to snakes. It is cold-blooded killing against targets that are seldom completely verified and who are almost always unaware they are in the crosshairs.

I get it. These are honorable servicemen using extraordinary skills to help America win battles. But honestly, what kind of emotional detachment is required to kill people like that? What do you tell yourself at the end of the day? How sure can you be the persons you killed were even combatants?

Please keep in mind I came by this attitude naturally. When you spend nearly a year of your life worrying about something, you are unlikely to embrace it in any fashion. I have read somewhere that the number one fear of American soldiers in Vietnam was snipers. Conscious fear, sub-conscious fear, it doesn't matter. It was one of those dark clouds that followed us every day. I know I was one of those soldiers who worried about snipers constantly.

The Viet Cong snipers had no trouble identifying us. We were big, round-eyed guys in uniforms. No confusion there. Radio guys like me even had long whip style antennas to call even more attention to ourselves. The mere thought of possible snipers was an effective tactic. It was a sub-category of terrorism that is obviously still working on a lot of us even today.

Nearly ten years after I left Vietnam, I found myself living in Beirut, Lebanon in the middle of a raging civil war. I was the Middle East Correspondent for NBC News. The war was truly a bitch to explain. It was the Christian right against the Moslem left but you could never forget that Palestinian refugees (Yasser Arafat's PLO) did most of the fighting for the Moslem side even though some of them were Christians. Got it? There were dozens of factions and each faction had its own private army and often its own foreign sponsors. Alliances shifted almost hourly.

Now that we've cleared that up I can tell you about the sniper nest my friend and photographer Jeff Riggins and I found one day in East Beirut on a hillside above the Tal Zaatar Palestinian refugee camp. This was at one point the largest of the refugee camps formed in 1948 when Arabs fled what is now Israel. At this time it had been under siege for months by Christian militias who wanted the refugees out of their portion of Beirut permanently.

The snipers were part of the Kataeb Christian private militia. They had set their position several stories up in a bombed out building about half a mile from the camp border. Their weapon of choice was a large, mounted .50 caliber machine gun set to fire single shots. It even had an attached springy chair to make their work easier. Their target area was a narrow slot between buildings residents had to cross to reach one of the last remaining water wells in Tal Zaatar.

The shooter was a smiling well-dressed guy in slacks and a white shirt. He and his friends had arrived in several fancy Range Rovers. It appeared there were enough people there for a good sized cheering section. And they did whoop it up every time they fired the gun.

By this point most of the PLO fighters had abandoned Tal Zaatar. It was a lost cause in any military sense. Most of the remaining residents were older people and children. They were the targets most of the time. We silently rooted for them every time someone made the quick dash to the well to get water to survive. This all became part of a story I did for NBC Nightly News that night and I am pleased to say no one was hit while we were there.

But the image of those fat cats laughing like jackals as they took pot shots into that camp has never left me. I promise there were many worse things that happened in that war on all sides but this is the picture that stuck in my craw. Along with my Vietnam experiences it really cemented my strong dislike of anyone associated with this type of warfare. I'm sure my old drill sergeant would have called me one of those politically incorrect words. But that's how I feel.

I can't find any reliable statistics on sniper deaths in Vietnam. I know we lost one of our platoon sergeants to a sniper in April of 1968 and possibly others I did not know about. As I have said, they were a constant menace. We had plenty of what we now call near misses.

So did I go to the movie "American Sniper?" No. Did that guy do anything worse than we did calling in artillery or air strikes? Maybe not. Was it any worse than shooting someone in a firefight? You decide. But as long as I'm writing this rant, I get the chance to let you know how I feel about snipers.

*November 18, 1967*

*Dear Mom,*

*I got your letter today about Reno and all and it sounds very interesting. I'm glad you are finally getting up the nerve to get around.*

*By the way, the reason you got three letters in one day is because they only take the mail off the ships twice a week and then when they get to our base camp at Dong Tam they only go out of there twice a week. Because of that my mail I send out can be delayed for as much as a week and come all at once. It's rather irritating but I'm sure they aren't going to change their system to suit me.*

*Your letter was the first letter I've received in a week except for a book from Marilyn and I'm beginning to wonder just what goes on — if any of my letters are getting through.*

[Note: Marilyn was pretty much the nicest person I had met in my life to that point. We had dated off and on the year before I went into the Army in a somewhat star-crossed way. She was a bright, pretty Mormon girl who was attending Brigham Young University. She was an amazingly good person. As smitten as I had been, I was still an untamable adventurer who had no plans to ever settle down and she knew that. Still, she wrote often and was a fun pen pal in those days. Her letters were greatly appreciated. I learned much later she had married young and had five kids. Twenty years later I had married and had four kids. I think we both did well.]

*As far as the fighting goes I'm sure you have a pretty good idea of the infantry's job but we haven't been into anything too serious since I've been here.*

*Tomorrow we go inland ever farther to a place called "Plain of Reeds" and that's right next to Cambodia. We'll be out about four days.*

*Also, skip the magazines but paperback books would be greatly appreciated. Also letters.*

*As far as my income goes, I make $120.00 a month base pay and $9.00 overseas pay and $65.00 combat pay. Out of this comes all the little nuisance deductions although I don't pay income tax and $75 for the savings bond. I might add that I'm long overdue for a raise that should be forthcoming in the next couple of weeks.*

*It sounds like Dick Fain is doing quite well these days and if you see him tell him hello for me and that I am sorry I wasn't able to see him while on leave.*

[Dick Fain was my old swim coach who had become

a family friend and a mentor to me. He became a high school principal and I looked up to him all my life.]

*Really, I don't want you to worry about me because I'm a pretty big boy now and quite capable of taking care of myself.*

*— Son William I*

*P.S. You will like SF also but the voice of experience can tell you most of the big niteclubs aren't worth the loot. $1.50 a drink—two drink minimum—poor drinks.*

Note: I seemed to know a lot about San Francisco bars in the sixties. Perhaps ID checks were not a strong point in those days.

# 12

# YOUR MAGIC SWIRLING SHIP

The following article was published in the *New York Times* prior to the completion of this book. It was a slightly modified version of the original chapter on helicopters and chopper pilots.

## *The Chopper Pilots*

WE WERE THE RIVER PEOPLE, but we also spent a lot of time on helicopters. I was a radio operator in the 9th Infantry Division, based in the Mekong Delta south of Saigon. By the time I left, someone told me I had made more than 50 combat assaults via chopper. Most but not all of them were routine insertions that could happen as often as three times in a day. Occasionally there was light resistance. A few times there was a good deal of shooting. And since you never really knew if and when the shooting would start, we all developed our own little formula for when, under fire, we would decide to jump out of the helicopter.

If I knew what a differential equation was, I would say this might have been one. There were so many variables. Foremost was altitude. You could jump from very high up and maybe break your legs. The forward speed of the chopper was something

Bill Lord as an infantryman in Vietnam.

to take into account. The landing area might be water, mud or dry land. All were factors. You wanted out of that chopper in the worst way because the chopper was the target. Still, you didn't want to get panicky and jump too soon. So each individual had his own leap point. Mine was probably about the height of jumping from the roof of a one-story house. Survivable and a good middle ground balancing all the risks.

The pilots did not have the luxury of jumping out. Helicopter pilots in Vietnam were among the hardiest of the whole bunch of us. They took a lot of casualties but they always seemed to be there when you needed them. Flying us into hot landing zones, flying medevacs to "dust off" the wounded and just getting potshots from all over when they were in the air meant there wasn't much in the way of a routine day for them. They earned every accolade they received. Many, too many, didn't survive: 2,165 helicopter pilots were killed in action, and another 2,500 crewmen.

Many of the survivors stuck with flying. Long after Vietnam those pilots often showed up to fly news helicopters for the television stations where I worked, and I loved to go flying with them. In uniform or out, these were very cool customers.

A helicopter is an awkward contraption. There are huge competing G-forces pulling in different directions, and it seems almost a miracle it can fly. It takes no small amount of skill to fly one even without the overlay of ground fire, steep landing zones and various life-or-death emergencies. And these pilots in Vietnam were never pampered.

We got a horrifying example of that one afternoon as we lined up to board choppers coming in to take us to the next landing zone. We were spread out in what were called pickets of six men each. Five groups were in a line on the left separated by about 25 yards each. Five more were on the right as the choppers descended onto our positions. You could figure out quickly which bird was coming for you and it was easy to follow it right to the ground. In this case as my eyes followed our chopper, I noticed a short length of barbed-wire fence just a couple of feet off the ground. It seemed too low to make any difference but the chopper came in a little fast, causing the pilot to lift the nose and drop the tail just enough for the tail rotor to hit that wire. The next events happened so fast it's hard to imagine even now how we survived.

At the moment the tail rotor hit the strand of wire, the chopper flipped onto its left side. The main rotor was driven into the ground and splintered into a thousand pieces. It was just our good fortune to have been on the right side of the chopper or we probably would not have survived. We had dived onto the ground but we could still see the right side door gunner and the co-pilot climbing out just as the now crashed chopper burst into flames. The co-pilot must have known that was going to happen because he exited the wreckage with a fire extinguisher. But it wasn't to put out the fire. The fire was already beyond that. He sprayed it directly on the plexiglass windshield in front of the pilot who was struggling to get out. The cold spray of carbon dioxide shrank the hot plastic and the windshield literally popped out. He pulled the pilot to safety as the fire raged.

The left-side door gunner never had a chance. He was pinned under the chopper right next to the fuel tank that was exploding into black smoke. By now we were all up and everyone thought to flip the burning chopper upright, but searing heat prevented us from getting near it. The gunner died very quickly.

The pilot was distraught beyond all description. Anyone would call this a tragic accident, but in his mind it was pilot error. In his mind his mistake had taken the life of one of his crew. There isn't much worse for a guy in his position.

It was a very bad scene. A smoldering chopper. A dead door gunner. Scared soldiers and this inconsolable pilot sitting on the ground wailing.

A few minutes into this drama several new choppers arrived on the scene, one carrying a guy who was clearly the man in charge of this whole chopper squadron. He was all business. He walked straight over to the pilot and told him to get up off the ground. He never asked what happened. No arm around the shoulder. He just walked the crying pilot over to the helicopter he had just arrived in and ordered the pilot to get in and take the stick.

The scene drove things home to us. This was a war. If you are going to be an effective pilot in the future, there is no time for grieving now. It was the ultimate version of getting back on the bicycle. But that's how they did things. There was no time for sentiment.

I met up not long ago with a former Vietnam chopper pilot who had been a few years ahead of me in our high school. He said it was the best job he ever had, despite all the dangers. He still missed it. As we talked I could tell that even now, 50 years later, he would happily get back in the cockpit. He still had that gritty commitment that reminded me of all the Vietnam pilots I had known. That's why we all trusted them with our lives.

Bill Lord is a retired television news executive and former general manager of WJ-LA-TV in Washington, D.C. During the Vietnam War he served as an infantry sergeant carrying a radio for Charlie Company, 4th/47 Infantry, 9th Infantry Division.

*Saturday, November 25, 1967*

*Dear Mom—*

*Would you believe that today, Saturday, is Thanksgiving? They made us go out to the woods on Thursday so when we got in today they gave us beer and turkey and proclaimed it Thanksgiving. About all it amounted to was a bunch of dipsomaniac G.I.'s fighting each other for no reason other than just to have a good time.*

*I got a letter from you and again you mentioned Fred-erick's. Please ignore Fredericks. All I want you can get at Tradewell and for a lot less loot. I appreciate the effort but smoked oysters just ain't my style.*

*I must admit I was shocked to hear about cousin Tom and I hope you will give me his address before he does anything definite. Tell him to volunteer for the draft and get into the Army and see what it's like before he decides on OCS because the opportunities are the same and if he changes his mind about it as I did he'll only have two years to do instead of three.*

[Note: My cousin Tom was a year older than I and was something of an idol when we were kids. He was smart and incredibly funny. We thought he was a sure bet to be a famous comedian. As it turned out, he went to Vietnam, experienced some awful things and had a hard time adjusting when he came home. Vietnam seemed to affect many aspects of his life. He died in a tragic motorcycle accident some years back but I have always believed his experiences in the Army played a major role in his later life.]

*As far as the National Guard goes, the standing joke around here is "I'd rather have a sister in a whorehouse than a brother in the National Guard."*

*I finally got a letter from Kathy after 14 months in the service and I answered it. I guess she's going to have another baby and doesn't seem to be minding too much.*

[Note: My sister having a second child at 21 was shocking to me. Interestingly, since I married so late her grandchildren are more the contemporaries of our kids.]

*Be sure and let me know how Reno was because I know if it was anything like Las Vegas you'll really enjoy it. You can even afford to go to the kind of places I had to gape at from the car windows.*

*In another couple of weeks we'll be moving off the ships and back to our base camp for six weeks which is a little more civilized except it gets mortared occasionally. At least they have a PX and a Snack Bar.*

*I got my official 9th Infantry Division Christmas Cards today and you'll be getting one whenever I get around to addressing and sending. They are a bit of a joke since they show a big wreath around a 9th Division shoulder patch but they're better than nothing.*

*Well Mom don't take too much loot off Boeing and take care of yourself. I think you should stage a heart attack in about February so I can come home for a month's emergency leave and then come back and go on R & R to Australia in late March or April.*

*Oh Well, I'll see you next September anyway and I'll be a proud civilian then.*

*Your Son,*
*The River Raider,*
*Audie Murphy*

# 13

# WORLD WAR Z

OKAY, TRUE CONFESSIONS. MY READING list is all over the map. My brain wanders. Sometimes that wandering results in odd or even amazing discoveries.

Long before *World War Z* was a troubled $200 million Brad Pitt movie it was actually a really well-written novel by a guy named Max Brooks. Max was born with some chops. He is the son of Mel Brooks and Anne Bancroft. *Brave New World* probably got me started on apocalyptic fiction back in the 60's so I guess going full Zombie made sense somehow.

*World War Z* was billed as An Oral History of the Zombie War. Buried in all this was a reference to a post-Vietnam song called "I Was Only 19." Most people probably read on past the reference. Many would probably believe a song mentioned in a Zombie novel would be some fictional invention. Not me. I have always been fascinated by our relative youth when we went to Vietnam. And when I saw the title "I Was Only 19" I had to check.

In the age of the Internet that was about a twenty second divot in my day as I searched YouTube and found it instantly. It's a song and

Aussie soldier in Vietnam from the Redgum video "I Was Only 19."

video from an Australian group called Redgum who I believe had covered an earlier version. But this video reached out and grabbed me. The combination of words, instrumentation and video captured the very essence of the Vietnam experience. It is the lament of a former soldier who started out young and proud and in the end was broken down by the relentless madness of the overall experience.

> *And can you tell me, doctor, why I still can't get to sleep?*
> *And night time's just a jungle dark and a barking M.16?*
> *And what's this rash that comes and goes, can you tell me*
>     *what it means?*
> *God help me - I was only nineteen*

I invite you to search this song and see if it has the same impact on you that it did on me. It may not. A colleague at work asked me not long ago the age old question "what was it like in Vietnam?" and I sent him a link. He wrote back, "I don't get it." Maybe you had to be there to really feel the anguish in the words about a soldier who dies just before he was scheduled to go home. And never forget how young we were. Do you know a nineteen year old kid? Think about it. Can you imagine him half a world away in combat surrounded by meaningless death and destruction? And ask yourself, do you call him a nineteen year-old man or a nineteen year old boy? That's what I try to get across about our youth.

> *And then someone yelled out "Contact", and the bloke*
>     *behind me swore*
> *We hooked in there for hours, then a God almighty roar*
> *And Frankie kicked a mine the day that mankind kicked*
>     *the moon*
> *God help me - he was goin' home in June.*

I'm also reminded of a banquet a few years back where I sat with WJLA-TV's veteran D.C. reporter Sam Ford. I used to tell people that Sam was my favorite passive aggressive person in the world. He would happily agree to anything you told him to do and would then go out and do exactly what he wanted to do. He's a great reporter and it was only because he came back with so many awesome stories he managed to get away with this friendly disobedience for the past thirty or so years.

That night he asked the usual series of unanswerable questions about Vietnam. What was it like? How did it change you? Do you still think about it now all these years later?

I finally came up with a truly honest answer that revealed a great deal while really saying almost nothing at all. I told him every time I hear a helicopter whomping across the sky I feel it right in pit of my stomach. It hits that little spot right between the ribs. And it's true. It's a physical reaction that can only be some tiny un-scrubbed adrenalin rush of fear associated with helicopters. Odd in that I still love flying in helicopters but real nonetheless. So I was also intrigued by this line in the Redgum song which had nothing to do with our Channel 7 at WJLA in Washington D.C. but still seemed to be on the same basic wavelength as my physical reaction.

> *And can you tell me, doctor, why I still can't get to sleep?*
> *Any why the Channel Seven chopper chills me to my feet?*
> *And what's this rash that comes and goes, can you tell me*
>     *what it means?*
> *God help me - I was only 19*

There are lots of memory triggers that take me back to Vietnam. The chopper sounds. The smell of diesel fuel. The slop of muddy river water. But really nothing grabs me like some of the songs that speak to the issues on a level many people would not even notice.

*November 30, 1967*

*Dear Mom —*

*Fatigue may prevent this from becoming too long and dull but I did want you to know I had received four packages of food, film and books. I'm expecting the record tomorrow since I assume they were ordered the same day.*

*In answer to your question, yes you can send larger cans about the size of a spaghetti can (with meat balls) and do send chili. The reason diminutive cans were stressed relates to the task of carrying them on my already overladen back.*

*We just returned from 4 ½ days and four nights of a rather exhausting nature. Last night, by far the worst of the lot, we experienced artillery rounds falling all around us because the Ground Surveillance Radar picked up a herd of water buffalo and, thinking they were VC, blasted away. We were so tired by then we laid in a ditch and laughed and told jokes and finally I got on my radio and had artillery fire illumination rounds for about half-hour so I could read my book and also because it kept the mosquitoes in line partially.*

*Anyway we finally staggered back aboard ship today, with all the sailors humming "From the Halls of Montezuma" much to our chagrin and I must say that at this point I feel nothing but respect for our Founder because I now know exactly how he must have felt on that seventh morning.*

*The books were excellent (especially the Twain and Kerouac) and I am now getting a good library stockpiled.*

*I already got Xmas from Boston in the form of a fine pipe to replace the one I foolishly left in a coffee house on Charles Street while I was slightly intoxicated and guilty of impersonating a hippie. Dad also sent a batch of books.*

*By the way, in what absurd fashion would you take pride in your son packing the radio? It really isn't any great honor and in my opinion thankless extra labor.*

*I'll write again soon and keep you informed of the latest mishaps and misfortunes.*

*Humbly I remain, your son in arms,*

*G.I. Emeritus,*
*Bill*

# 14

# THE ENEMY

OUR ENEMY WAS THE VIET Cong. The V.C. Victor Charlie. Charlie. Even Chuck sometimes. We hated the V.C. We killed them. We called them racist names. We referred to them as gooks, usually with an F-word modifier. If there was an American in Vietnam who did not call the Viet Cong gooks I didn't meet him or her. And there is no falling back on the fact gook is the Korean word for person. When we used that word it was a racial insult.

Yet, here's where it gets odd. We did respect the Viet Cong. Sure, we hated them. They were the enemy. But we never underestimated them. They were physically tough. They could endure all measures of hardship. They were highly motivated because they were fighting for their lives in their own rice paddies. They were courageous. Their guerilla warfare tactics were very effective at tying up huge numbers of Americans. They were certainly not to be taken lightly.

The big problem was trying to identify who actually was a Viet Cong. It was easy if they had a gun but that wasn't always the case. And here's the rub. Every company commander in Vietnam tended to have a different idea about rules of engagement. Some

were clearly way out of line as in the My Lai Massacre. But there were many other shades of gray. Almost all the people we encountered were very probably Viet Cong sympathizers if they weren't actively involved with the Viet Cong. Our rule in Charlie Company, to the best of my knowledge, was you could only shoot an actual armed combatant except in extreme circumstances.

Case in point. One day we were working our way up a trail through a wooded area and about twenty feet ahead of our point man, a young guy pops out of the bushes, takes one look at our team and takes off running in the other direction. He was about twenty, wearing the standard black pajama type pants and looked like a poster child for a Viet Cong soldier. But he had no apparent weapon. Our point man shot him dead.

Justified or not? Think about it. He could very well have been part of a larger group preparing to ambush our unit. He might have shown himself completely by accident after leaving his weapon in a bunker. Then again, he could have been walking home from school and got startled by bumping into American soldiers. What's the right answer? The guy who did the shooting was upset. He had just killed someone and he thought he might be in trouble.

This was cleared up quickly. The first officer who showed up took one look at what had happened and said something very much like this, "Fuck it, the guy shouldn't have been here. He's V.C. This is a good shooting. No problem."

So this became what we called a "sorry about that" moment where nobody was going to dig up the facts. You looked suspicious, you were in a bad place and you got shot. Sorry about that.

Believe me, there were no civilian review boards in Vietnam. The fact we even discussed this briefly indicates our company as far more conservative than most. There were many, many troop commanders in Vietnam who had a shoot first and ask questions later policy. Assume everyone is a Viet Cong. Shoot anybody you see that looks suspicious. Now define suspicious. Everybody had a different standard. You get the idea. A lot of people got shot for looking suspicious. Questions were extremely rare. If anyone was killed by accident they were automatically declared Viet Cong. A lot of soldiers appreciated the shoot first policy because it seemed safer. A lot of commanders liked it because it improved their body count, the coin of the realm in Vietnam. A lot of Battalion Commanders liked the body counts because it gave them something they could distort like a Jimi Hendrix amplifier.

Bottom line, Charlie was a tough enemy. He really was tough to kill. He was motivated. And there's one more thing the American side totally failed to notice. Most of the Viet Cong were not sophisticated enough to really understand communism and embrace it. In their minds they were simply Vietnamese. They were essentially Vietnamese nationalists following Ho Chi Minh who in their minds was an inspirational leader. The communist label was a convenient one for us to use to isolate them from any negotiations but in the end most of them would probably have said they were just fighting for their country. They were, in their minds, patriots.

*December 8, 1967*

*70 S.E. of Saigon Near Cambodia*
*Dear Mom,*
    *You really won at Reno? Hard to believe.*
    *I paid for my 9th Division yearbook ($7.50) and it should be mailed to your address. If it isn't there by April let me know and I get my money back.*

*Did you get my fabulous Christmas card with the 9th Division shoulder patch wrapped up in a nice wreath? That must be some sort of sacrilege at least.*

[Note: Compliments of the Internet I was able to find this card.]

*I was awarded (well, almost everyone gets one so it's not much of an award) my Combat Infantryman's Badge today. Swell. I've always been dying to have one.*

[Note: I made light of this at the time but from the perspective of all these intervening years I can honestly say it is the one piece of Army hardware I actually hold in high esteem. It sort of sets you apart as a real soldier. Even though I came to oppose the war during my time there, I'm proud of it. It's given to the guys who answered the call regardless of the circumstances.]

*I guess we go back out tomorrow up near (too near) the Cambodian border again but after last time I'm sure old "Mr. Charles" is too weak to mess with us.*

*The rest of the war is about the same. I go up on the bow of the ship and blow pot and listen to records (I'm still waiting for "Fire") with the rest of the boys and do my best to enjoy my misery in any possible way.*

*If you go to Frisco be sure to go to the "Peppermint Tree" on Broadway & Grant. They give you about the best drinks and have a Snake Lady that does a topless act with a boa constrictor. Whatever you do, don't buy mixed drinks. We did once and they were terrible after that we switched to rum with a coke backer and thusly guaranteed at least a shot for our buck and a half.*

*I don't think you'll want to hit all the topless joints because like the old saying goes, "you seen one you seen 'em all" but do hit old "Finnochios" once to believe it.*

[Note: I'm a little bewildered that I knew so much about San Francisco bars. I think I was only there for a week or so but I must have remembered every little thing.]

*Also if you ever see any more books by Jack Kerouac sent them post haste.*

*I'll drop off now. Take it easy and enjoy yourself Xmas.*

*Your Son the Plunderer,*
*Bill*

# 15

# SNOOPY'S NOSE

"Okay guys, we're heading back to Snoopy's Nose," Bob Nardel-li said happily at four in the morning as we boarded our landing craft for another three-day so-called search and destroy mission. "This is gonna be fun."

It's hard to recall dialogue all these years later but I'm sure someone, probably me, would have said something derisive about Bob's mother. Unbridled cheeriness is not always welcome as you stumble through the foggy transition from deep sleep to combat readiness.

"The only thing worse than a mean drunk is a friendly one," I always told Bob. "And the same is true of soldiers."

"The only thing worse than a grumpy soldier at four in the morning is a happy one."

Our loading plan was a slow steady process of working through our personal checklists in sticky humid darkness. Generally we were

on a barge alongside the troop ship Benewah preparing to board our landing craft, the Tango boats. We filled canteens, loaded weapons and stowed extra ammo. Nardelli and I were radio guys so we were blessed with twenty extra pounds of equipment, batteries, spare headsets and the like. C-Rations came in feeble little cardboard boxes. We stripped them open and stuffed all the cans into spare socks we hung off the back of our pack frames. You needed about a quarter pound of C-4 explosive to cook and a P-38, the ubiquitous inch long can opener we all lost almost daily. We often choose between a poncho and an air mattress for the over nights but it didn't really matter. You were going to be wet and miserable either way. The poncho weighed a little less and as such was more popular.

These rituals were generally silent unless someone like Nardelli wanted to talk smack about the Dodgers or some such irrelevant crap. Imagine sleepy-eyed debates on the relative merits of California versus Texas to add to the irritation factor. Total mindlessness.

Let's face it. Nardelli was seemingly the happiest guy in Vietnam. He was upbeat and joking almost all of the time. He approached our plight like he was cruising up the Pacific Coast Highway with the top down in his home town of Redondo Beach, California. He was eighteen. He had what he called his "sort of" girlfriend who wrote regularly and he was making the best of a bad situation. Unlike many of us he did not strive to get home and get to college. He wanted to get home to the beach and hang out with his buddies. Most of the time having a good-natured kid nearby was really entertaining. A little dial back in the morning would have been okay too, though.

Being happy to go to Snoopy's Nose again was way out on the edge of nuts. This was an area alongside a meandering tributary of the Mekong River shaped exactly like the nose of the cartoon dog.

It had become a legendary cute map feature. There was no end to the jokes and chatter. It was memorable but the bottom line though is that it was a mean ass place. You have to remember that when we slogged through rice paddies it was hot, miserable and incredibly dull work. We could go many days and sometimes more where absolutely nothing happened. And then in an instant the boredom could shatter.

That was what was so annoying about Snoopy's Nose. The boredom always seemed to shatter there. It was seldom anything horrible, but bad stuff nonetheless. Long range snipers to scare everyone. Booby trap areas. Little one and two person ambushes where the shooters would just evaporate after firing off a few rounds. There was a lot of monotony to what we did but that's not how we liked to break it.

Later that day after the Tango boats inserted us upstream without incident (honestly, I think it was that day but it may have another) we were approaching a tree line and some buildings on the edge of the stream. Our guys were fanned out across a flooded rice paddy. On the left were the usual farmer hootches we saw every day but on the right was an actual building. It appeared to be an old monastery or something left over from the French or some previous occupier. In this setting it appeared so oddly out of place that it could be a watercolor painting on the wall of some Saigon bar. That's guess work. I never saw a Saigon bar. Or Bob Hope. I did meet one Donut Dolly along with ten other guys very briefly in a Navy mess hall. But I digress.

Nardelli and I had a pretty good view of our operation that day from behind because we were the radio guys for the company commander. My job was to relay orders to the various platoon leaders up in front of us and to stay in contact with an army colonel flying above us in an observation chopper. Radio call sign Delta Devil 6. Never knew his name. Nardelli was the forward artillery observer so when we got into trouble he was on a separate artillery frequency and would direct the fire of artillery batteries ten miles away. His job was to hit the bad guys and more important than that to avoid hitting us. It was exacting work for an 18 year-old. He did it well. These two radioman jobs had us pretty much attached at the hip 24 hours a day when we were in the field.

Anyway as we gazed out across this scene that day something triggered a mental alarm. About fifteen guys were moving forward like picket fence posts toward an area that afforded good cover to anyone wanting to do us harm. Remember, this was the exact situation Captain Lind warned about after June 19th. Nardelli and I let the company commander know this and he stopped the entire advance and ordered a standard two-person point patrol to get out in front of the group. The job of the point people is to find the danger before it could create lots of casualties for a larger group. Having large numbers of people out in the open was a terrible tactical error and we almost paid dearly for it.

Within just a minute or two the shooting started.

When this happens out in the open you really only have two choices. You can make a break for a foot high dike separating the race paddies or you can hunker in place. Hunker is such a great word. It may sound like you're just lying there but in this context hunker is a very active verb. You are in the act of hunkering in dung-colored water and mud until nary a butt cheek is showing on the horizon. So we hunkered.

As time went by it became clear this was yet another Snoopy's Nose harassment attack. There were really just three or four bursts of automatic weapons fire from far enough out that no one was hit.

Whoever did the shooting was long gone by the time we got our act together to de-hunker and more forward. We found some shell casings later but we couldn't even be sure they were related to this shooting. All we got out of this was a twenty second terror break interrupting the boredom and then more boredom.

Except for Nardelli. You should have heard him.

"Hey, we just saved the day," he said with a beaming smile. "That could have been a terrible ambush and we should get medals for seeing that coming and putting out the warning."

He went on.

In fact, he was joking. He was always joking. We deserved nothing. But the story did have something of a moral to it. Honestly, you just couldn't ever let your guard down. Situations like that sometimes did lead to casualties. And if you ever let the monotony cause you to hurry across the rice paddy so you might get a smoke break in the shade, you might end up very sorry. That's why the relentless stress and pressure ate at a lot of guys as much as the actual combat.

So. Snoopy's Nose. Danger, stress and pressure. Every time.

And Nardelli. The only guy I ever knew who could say Vietnam really sucks….with a smile on his face.

*December 21, 1967*

*Dong Tam, R.V.N.*
*Dear Mom —*

*I guess I really haven't been very regular at corresponding of late but "The War" has kept me very busy. We had three operations right together and then moved off the ships and back into our base camp here at Dong Tam. As soon as I got here I was put on perimeter guard which was two days ago and "Old Reliable" Bill is still sitting here on Bunker #16 basking in the sunshine.*

*This is the real easy job since you just sit out here and listen to the radio and drink Cokes all day.*

*Yesterday they let us off for awhile and we went to the PX and Snack Bar. I got my first hamburger since I got to Viet Nam (very poor I might add). It is funny sounding but it was the first time in the last 2 ½ months that I had walked on dry ground without my pack and M-16.*

Guarding the perimeter at Dong Tam. Number of ground attacks in my time there: Zero. BTW the 9th Division was called the "Old Reliables," hence the reference above.

*The immediate future looks to be more perimeter guard and running patrols in the general area about the base camp which is a real vacation from the stuff we've been doing.*

*Our barracks leave a little to be desired since some fool built them next to a battery of 155mm artillery guns and every time the artillery fires the lights fall out of the sockets due to the building shaking so much.*

[Note: They often fired these artillery guns in the wee hours of the morning. I have no idea what they might have been targeting but I do know this. There will never be a wake-up call to ever rival this one. Literally, the extreme noise and concussion from these guns would lift you up from the bunk and drop you back down. Your resting heart beat seemed to leap from sixty beats a minute to a hundred or more. Believe me you don't wake up groggy. You wake all the way up instantly spiked with adrenaline and looking for the bear you might have to wrestle.]

*I guess I will be here for six weeks or so and after that probably back to the ships and regular operations. There is a rumor that 9th Division Headquarters will move to Dong Tam and that the Mobile Riverine Force or 2nd Brigade (which is us) will move deeper into the Delta and establish a new base camp in the area of the Cam Son Secret Zone where all our recent operations have been. This would be sort of interesting to be able to start something and watch its progress as one became a "Short Timer."*

*McLeod was finally kicked out of the Naval Academy for breaching the Honor Code which is to say he neglected to turn in a friend for some misdemeanor and frankly I think as far as Honor is concerned his actions were entirely correct. I imagine he feels bad but apparently still has his sense of humor. He signed his last letter:*

*Midshipman 3/C, Retired*

[Note: My college roommate John McLeod had the misfortune of having his Naval Academy room-mate sneak a girl into the barracks. John politely left the room (my college kids always referred to this as being sexiled). John's roommate tried to lie his way out of it all. John says he refused to point the finger at him and for that he was dismissed.]

*I hope you enjoy S.F. but remember what I told you about getting cheated on things there. I'll send this to your hotel and hope you get it.*

*Say hello to all our California type relatives and I hope you had a nice Xmas.*

*Your Son,*
*William*

*P.S. Bob Hope won't be coming to Dong Tam because we're infantrymen and he'll be busy putting on shows for the "Remington Rangers" in Saigon.*

Note: There was another rude slogan for non-infantry types. REMF's. Rear Echelon Motherfuckers.

# 16

# CHRISTMAS EVE, 1967

A HOLIDAY TRUCE SEEMED TO me a strange thing in the middle of a war. Let's all take a little time out, have a nice dinner and then get back to killing each other next Monday. In Vietnam that was a three-day pass from reality.

The Christmas truce of 1967 was the real deal. It was before the Tet Offensive, back when a truce was really a truce. All the American units came in from the field. I guess Charlie went back to his hootch and had a nice fish and rice stew. The whole country just went quiet and that didn't feel right at all. It maybe didn't feel right but certainly there were no complaints. Three days of no shooting meant a slight uptick in the odds of survival until DEROS, the army way of saying Date Eligible for Return from Overseas or more simply, going home. Everybody was a math major in Vietnam.

I guess it was just bad luck that our company got fingered to pull base security on Christmas Eve. There were twenty or so reinforced sand-bagged bunkers around our perimeter housing big machine guns and

Here I am guarding our sad little attempt at a Christmas tree out on the Dong Tam perimeter.

generally manned at night with somewhere between four and six soldiers each. Our job was to keep an eye out for anyone trying to overrun the base by crossing a large open area of "no man's land" before we could shoot them. No one had ever tried this before and it was unlikely anyone would try in the middle of the Christmas truce. This was going to alter our drinking plans for the night but as it turned out it didn't kill them completely.

We began smuggling beer and whiskey late in the afternoon. That required some scrounging because party coolers were in short supply and ice had a very short shelf life in the Vietnam climate. We were not deterred. I am just guessing there were also smoking components to what was shaping up to be a party but I really don't remember. It was Christmas, right?

George Scott and another Oklahoma boy named Fink (that's Fink on the bottom) were right in the middle of all this. I believe they had a hand in finding history's scrawniest Christmas tree which was immediately festooned with decorative C-Ration cans. They were great ambassadors from the state of Oklahoma and a few years later when Senator Dewey Bartlett made me an Honorary Okie for some student reporting I did on Capitol Hill I would have loved to have shown them my certificate.

Let me just say things kept getting more relaxed as the evening wore on and several of the perimeter guards began visiting back and forth among all the bunkers. No one really claimed credit for this idea but it slowly developed after one drink became two drinks and so on. This guard duty was not complicated stuff. If someone tries to run toward you across several hundred yards of empty sand it would be prudent to shoot them. It would also be prudent to let everyone else know what was going on.

To that end each of the bunkers was well supplied with flares. White flares provided illumination, red flares signified a ground attack and green flares signified a mortar attack on our base. The big thinkers in the group, and I won't name names, noted what lovely Christmas colors those were and how beautiful they might look flying across the night sky at say midnight on Christmas Eve.

Alcohol flowed. Word spread. Midnight arrived.

A red flare went off on the western perimeter first triggering a quick response from the Base Command Center which was not in our little plan.

"What's going on out there, guys?" the radio chirped.

By then green flares were going off in the north and east. White flares started going off all over. More reds would soon follow and before you knew it the Christmas light show we had intended was in full effect. It was beautiful.

Then the Command Center engaged the air raid siren. That meant everyone on the base had to get up and move to an underground bunker.

"We have ground and mortar fire around the perimeter. We're getting reinforcements. Call in... we need more information now," we were hearing on the radio.

We had another little problem. We were intoxicated and all laughing so hysterically we were exceptionally poor witnesses. They caught on quickly. The next voice we heard on the radio was a sleepy and incredibly pissed off colonel who tongue lashed us over the radio beyond all measure. I wish I could remember the exact things he said but I can only recall a few words. Remember, a good military ass-chewing was a significant art form. This guy had obviously practiced for twenty years or so.

Stupid Motherfuckers was a phrase he used liberally. Court-Martial every dumbass one of you was another. Personally come out there and kick your ass had to have been in there somewhere. I am reasonable sure we were too drunk to care.

Finally, all the flares burned out and inexplicably the colonel did too.

At the end of it all he got a little quieter.

"Okay," he said. "You've had your fun. Now get back to guard duty."

And after a long pause.

"Merry Christmas."

*December 27, 1967*
*Dear Mom,*

*I received your package on Christmas Day and your letter today. The package was just what I've been wanting all along. Just add cashews and we're uptight. I shared the chili with my two regular cohorts for Xmas dinner since we were in the field. Although obviously adverse conditions we really did have sort of a good time on the Eve and day.*

*Also today I received a nice card from the Jordans and also the annual $5 from Minner.*

[Note: The Jordans were my aunt, uncle and cousins from California. On several occasions they awakened to find me and my traveling companions sleeping in their front yard during our trips up and down the coast. If they found this irritating they concealed it well and always showed us a good time. Minner was my grandmother who sent us a crisp five dollar bill in one of those little pocket cards every year for Christmas and our birthdays.]

*I haven't decided the fate of it yet since we only use Military Payment certificates here and US Currency is strictly taboo. I think I'll keep it in my wallet as my own little personal rebellion against constant harassing authority. I'll answer them soon. I got 7 letters today and I'm trying to get some answered tonight.*

*I imagine you've returned from S.F. and I hope all went.*

*Tell your friend Joan, if she isn't too busy carousing around to make up another batch of cookies but please, please, spare me the burden of trying to give away the bourbon balls or whatever that candy was. I'm serious, the (local kids) wouldn't even eat them.*

*A sergeant in our squad left for home yesterday while we were in the field (he completed his year) and when we got back he had left with my name and a friend of mine named George Scott written along with Merry Xmas on a bottle of J.W. Dant Bourbon which is a real prize around here. Not a fifth mind you, but an Imperial Quart.*

[Note: We didn't really know much about hard liquor so we liberated a can of concentrated grapefruit juice from the mess hall. We were going to make "mixed drinks." Very sophisticated and all. Not only did it taste terrible, it seemed to make us all feel pretty sickly. The next morning we read the instructions which said to mix the contents of the concentrated grapefruit can with TWENTY GALLONS of water. We drank the Bourbon straight after that fiasco. And I have avoided grapefruit juice ever since.]

*Well, again exhaustion is making heavy eyes and it's late. They are really not giving me much time to write these days but I'll do my best.*

*Your #1 Son,*
*Bill*

# 17

# MANAGEMENT 101

I NOW JOKE WITH PEOPLE that I learned everything I needed to know about managing people as an infantry sergeant in Vietnam. I'll confess now it isn't really a joke. For the last 35 years I have managed large TV newsrooms and at times entire television stations. I was always guided by three principles. Be decisive. Be honest. And always, always look after your people.

There is a brilliant scene in the Vietnam movie Full Metal Jacket. As I recall it a squad gets pinned down in some urban area. The enemy has them pinpointed so if they stay put they will almost certainly be killed. Retreat is a bad option because there's no cover. A move to the left has some cover but no one knows what's over there. A move to the right seems like it would be moving somewhat toward the incoming fire.

What do these guys have to do with this story? You'll see.

The squad leader has to make a decision very quickly. He has to be honest enough to let people know the options or lose all credibility. And he has to communicate that he is making a decision in the best interest of all of them.

Life and death decisions in the heat of a war don't get repeated in the business world but they certainly are instructive. All my life I have made dozens of decisions every day that required rapid responses based on too little information. Television news is a "right now" sort of business. Almost always no decision is the worst decision. So you assess the situation as best you can and make the call as quickly as you can. Tell people the truth about why you are doing what you are doing and always let it be known that you believe it's the best course for the team.

Case in point. The Devil himself would have been proud to create this little scenario. The jury was out deliberating in the OJ Simpson Civil Trial. I was the news director at KNBC in Los Angeles. The criminal jury had already acquitted OJ in his first trial. We had spent months preparing our coverage for the results of this one. Our brilliant special projects guy Peter O'Connell spent weeks scouting all the locations learning where each party would be after the verdict and setting up live camera positions. We were prepared and confident we could go into live coverage and win the day in this enormously competitive media market. We were, pardon the expression, locked and loaded. Except for one little thing.

President Bill Clinton was delivering his State of the Union speech that night. Man that guy could talk. On the West Coast the speech started at 6pm. We had assumed the jury would break for dinner and there would be no conflict. Inexplicably the jury decided to work straight through indicating the decision may be close. As the speech went on we started getting more and more nervous. I stood in front of a bank of literally dozens of live monitors prepared to direct the live coverage.

Cameras were banned from the courthouse we so had an elaborate system to get the information out. There were seven counts and as each one was read out with a verdict a runner would leave the media room with a sign saying "Count One GUILTY" (or the opposite) and hold it up to a window where an outdoor camera could see it. Another outdoor camera was trained on our reporter in another part of the courthouse who was prepared to do commentary over her cell phone. Hey, they said no cameras. They didn't think to ban cell phones and shooting through the windows.

At about the one hour mark of Clinton's speech things got dicey. The jury was coming back into the courtroom. Clinton showed no signs of letting up. Shit, shit, shit.

Up until this point I don't think any television station in America had ever really thought of dumping the President of the United States to go to a local news story. It may sound silly now but we didn't have secondary channels. In those days we had one pipeline and the President pretty much owned it for the State of the Union. He was on all the cable channels as well. But I started thinking about dumping out of the speech. Several people said it was heresy. Others said come on man, let's do it. My boss was with me and saw what I was thinking. She was at the top of any class in company politics. She said it was up to me to take the fall if things went wrong.

By now Clinton was talking about windmills in Luxembourg or something. He was an hour and ten minutes in and counting. Word from the press room was that the jury was back seated in the courtroom.

I think my exact quote was something like, "what the heck,

dump the President, go to the anchors and toss to OJ." I may also have been thinking "what are they going to do, send me to Vietnam?" Memory fades.

In rapid succession the President was bumped in mid-sentence. The Breaking News banner played and our anchors tossed to the courthouse in time to see the first shot in the window, the banner proclaiming "Count #1 GUILTY." OJ Simpson was convicted in a civil trial of murdering his wife. We had at least scooped the world on that one.

We watched our competitors. KCBS stayed with the speech. About halfway through the reading of the counts KABC must have seen what we were doing and tried a half measure. They kept up the President's speech but showed an unexplained insert shot of their verdict window. That made us happy because we knew anyone wanting OJ coverage would start looking for it and would only find it on KNBC. We were off to the races.

So this was a hard call and to my knowledge and unprecedented call under a lot of pressure in the TV world. But it matched up to my three principles pretty well. It was decisive. The safe choice was do nothing and play catch up. It was honest because I had to be the one who said our audience wants the OJ verdict and not more President Clinton. And it really looked after our guys. I don't think I could have looked them in the eye if I let all that preparation go wasted because I didn't have the balls to pull the plug on the President.

Maybe it seems like an obvious call now but it was seriously radical at the time. I didn't know if I would get a call from GE President Bob Wright the next day telling me to pack up or if I would be hailed as a programming wizard. I should have guessed nobody was going to say a word without the benefits of the overnight rating results to guide their level of outrage. It wouldn't be the first time hypocrisy gently crept into broadcast management. And as it turned out, I was saved by the numbers.

In the first five minutes of OJ coverage KNBC's ratings increased three-fold. As the night wore on ratings continued to climb as our massive preparation effort was executed perfectly. Every time a lawyer or a family member or a juror wanted to say something a KNBC live camera was right there. We ended up with more viewers than all the other stations combined.

Did surviving the pressures of Vietnam help with this and many other decisions I have made over the years? Absolutely. Even if it was just that vague awareness that timely decisions were really important. Yes. Even when I was wrong which happened often enough, at least we were on the move rather than being beaten by inaction. The guys in Full Metal Jacket made an uncomfortable choice and somehow they survived. With far less at stake, we did too. Finally, if they sat me in a conference room full of bosses to yell at me the next day I was damn sure none of them would have guns. Vietnam gave me that advantage, too. It's always been hard to intimidate me without pointing a gun in my direction.

This may sound silly now but I know a lot of people who look at business decisions as life and death matters. That's almost never the case. They are mere shadows of life and death decisions. If you have made those types of decisions in a combat setting you are very well prepared to make the right choices as a civilian. It worked for me my entire professional life.

*January 2, 1967*
*Dear Mom—*

*Well, it's been quite awhile since I've written but they've had me in the field since Xmas morning and we had sort of a hard time. I celebrated your birthday by jumping out of a*

*helicopter on a hot L.Z. or landing zone and we proceeded to*
*engage in about a 24 hour firefight that wasn't too pleasant.*
*We stayed two and a half days in a pagoda (bombed out) in*
*a little village for the New Year's Truce and all day on Jan.*
*1st I divided my time decoding the pro-football scores com-*
*ing in on the radio and sitting in the pagoda before Buddha,*
*cross-legged reading that Kerouac book about Dharma on*
*the "True Meaning." I finally concluded that one would be*
*wasting his life to chase around mountain tops searching for*
*this nonsense of "Truth" and whatever. It was sort of nice to*
*fool around like that anyway.*

[Note: The games on the radio referenced remind
me of an evil little trick I played on one of my colleagues during the World Series. The games were
broadcast on Radio Saigon during the afternoon.
This seemed a little improbable to me due to the
eleven hour time difference between Saigon and
the East Coast. I did just a tiny bit of investigating
and found that they were indeed playing the game
on a delay. I then went somewhere to find out the
actual score before quite confidently betting one
of my fellow soldiers five dollars on the outcome
of the game. I have no idea now what teams were
playing. Anyway, my team miraculously pulled off
the victory and he was ready to pay up. In the end
I didn't take the money. It was actually more fun to
explain the time difference and the delayed broadcast to him than it was to take his money. He face
just sort of fell unhappily as I explained to him that
he had been rascaled.]

*There have been times recently that I feel like I have just*
*about reached my capacity for fear, exhaustion, hate, hope*

*and grief yet for some reason the next day it's all over and just one big joke. Anyway these next eight months are looking to be awfully long.*

*We were supposed to get sort of a break and pull this Base Camp Security for 6-8 weeks but it lasted about 5 days before they started sending us out again and it's getting worse rather than better.*

*I have a new job now. I started out with my squad leader's radio, then to my platoon leader's radio and as of today I begin carrying my company commander's radio. This means I have an outside chance to make sergeant before I'm through with this mess which means little but I'd like the loot.*

*I'm so mixed up and rushed around I don't know if I thanked you for the Xmas package or not but it was great, send more.*

*I must answer some more letters, since I've been too busy to lately. Take care of yourself and don't worry about*

*Your Son,*
*William H.*

# 18

# FORTUNATE SON

I ALWAYS CONNECTED TO CREEDENCE Clearwater songs even before Vietnam but nothing that compares to my connection with the song "Fortunate Son." It came out not long after I got back. John Fogerty of Creedence had written a song that really spoke to circumstance in my case. By the time I got back I had achieved a level of cynicism to believe there really was one group of privileged Americans who had talked tough and sent people to war and then my group, whoever we were, who went off to fight the war.

> *Some folks are born made to wave the flag*
> *Ooh, they're red, white and blue*
> *And when the band plays "Hail to the chief"*
> *Ooh, they point the cannon at you, Lord*

As it turned out Vietnam was a lot more difficult than either group ever imagined. Still, in a very quiet way this song became a profound personal anthem for me. It was a little chip I wore on my shoulder my whole life even though no one had

John Fogerty sings "Fortunate Son" at Wolftrap, VA, 2015. My son and I were in the front row and got this picture.

any idea it was there. It was my way of separating the people who talked tough and the people who could really do the tough work. I know this sounds juvenile but it worked for me.

As time went on the song seemed almost prophetic. After 9/11 George Bush and Dick Cheney were hell bent on kicking some Arab butt. Never mind they both had done everything possible to avoid actually getting in harm's way during Vietnam. They were happy to send others to Iraq based on bogus information about weapons of mass destruction. They had reduced our national defense efforts to the level of a high school football game and sent our guys out there to the cheers of millions. We had been attacked. We needed to fight back. Did it really matter who we fought back against? Apparently not. Remember that ill-fated "Mission Accomplished" speech. We lost four thousand honorable American lives so Bush and Cheney could sit in DC and talk tough like that.

> *Some folks inherit star spangled eyes*
> *Ooh, they send you down to war, Lord*
> *And when you ask them, "How much should we give?"*
> *Ooh, they only answer More! more! more! yoh*

No one honors those Iraq and Afghanistan soldiers more than Vietnam veterans. And many Vietnam veterans do not share my view that the war in Iraq was contrived to win political advantages for Bush and Cheney. But are there two groups? One group talks tough and sends in the troops. The other group is made up of the ones who serve. I think yes. And I think "Fortunate Son" captures that notion in a powerful way.

In his book "Fortunate Son" John Fogerty says he wrote the song in about twenty minutes. It was about privilege. He may have been simply referring to the privileged people who avoided service in

Vietnam. I took it beyond that. It was people who avoided service but still waved the flag and sent others into battle. That grated on me then and it grates on me now. Donald Trump is our current tough talker who wants to send people into battle. He can't even remember which foot he claimed had bone spurs to get out of serving during Vietnam.

Even though I was a "boss" for thirty some years, I always managed down. I always identified with the people who were doing the work rather than the privileged people calling the shots. To the very end I had problems managing up. I connect that distinction to my life as a grunt in Vietnam and to my appreciation of "Fortunate Son."

*January 20. 1968, Dong Tam*
*Dear Mom,*

*I got your letter one day and your portfolio the next so I figured I better get back on the writing stick. We are pulling security for our base camp for awhile so everything is quite easy for the time being.*

*If I don't forget, there should be two enclosures to this great essay. First, one of your maps with some pertinent information on it and secondly a picture of your number one son, taken just before Xmas.*

*The pictures of the R & R centers were quite nice and although all these oriental exotics are tempting I still am hanging on for Australia which will be more expensive but rich with round-eyed English speaking female personnel. I am going to have to wait until June but it should be worth it.*

[Note: I apologize for my younger self if this sounds racist. I think I was longing for Western Civilization more than anything else.]

*I'm trying to negotiate a deal which would allow me to go in March but I can't tell yet.*

*As far as this asinine war goes I guess I do feel differently than I did when I left but I still feel that we should be here. My main objections are the way we are misinformed, the public is brainwashed by totally imaginary statistics and I think most of all the way some colonel can fly around in a helicopter and play checkers with my life. This last objection is an occupational hazard I realize, but they let the senile warped old men run this show and they love it. This war will never end as long as there is a general in the U.S. Army because playing with their map tacks is what they have been longing for all their lives and they have no conception of what is going on down in the mud because they rarely leave their air conditioned bunkers or, in totally secure areas where most of them are, air conditioned offices.*

*Certainly we still have an obligation here however we seem to lack the capacity to fulfill the obligation due to these career hat-racks. Their idea of a pacification program is to feed the Viet Cong, patch up the civilians they destroy with their foolish inaccuracies and shortsightedness.*

[Note: I notice I am still keeping alive this notion of us having an obligation in Vietnam. By now I had ample evidence that we were engaged in a monumental mistake and yet I did not seem to push this notion in my letters home. I wrote about all the issues but not yet to the point of saying we needed to get out.]

*As for my personal mission as I see it I plan to avoid any part of the war I can, finish my year and come home and forget it. I still will do my job (quite well I might add) but I'm not going out of my way to do anything other than keep my young body in one big beautiful piece.*

*As far as packaged goods, cashews and chocolate chip cookies, more chili and maybe more spaghetti and meat balls. Send it soon because I am losing weight at an alarming rate.*

*Why don't you buy a big house (or a little one) in the "U" District and when I get back I'll rent it from you and you can get an apartment farther north? Sound good?*

*Well, I'll see you later,*
*Bill*

# 19

# FRIENDLY FIRE

TAKE A LOOK AT THIS guy. He's a central character in a story I would sometimes tell when my kids demanded to hear something about Vietnam. He was a career Army sergeant and in my view in those days an "old guy." I doubt he was thirty yet but that made him Barcalounger ready in our book. He was a good guy. He managed to split the difference between being a by the book soldier and a having a soft spot for sorry ass draftee grunts like us.

You could argue with him as I did one morning about why on this particular day someone had ordered us all to carry entrenching tools on this specific mission. An entrenching tool is a shovel with a military name. I believe I told him that the shovel was as useless as boobs on a bull in the Mekong Delta or something like that.

"You can't dig a hole. The water table is about a foot below dry land," I argued.

"The Army wants you to have that with you," he countered.

"It would be better to carry a bag of rocks. We could throw them."

A great Platoon Sergeant whose name has escaped me. I believe the child was just a prop for the photo. I have a lot of old photos like this.

It went on. He smiled. In the end, I packed up the shovel like everyone else.

Fast forward many hours and we found ourselves in what the Army called a "blocking position." We were strung out along a canal to make sure no Viet Cong would be able to "escape" across that canal from other American units that might be pursuing them. For guys who hiked for miles with 50 pounds of gear on their backs, we had another word for "blocking position." We called it heaven. We sat in the shade, ate chocolate C-rations, smoked cigarettes and caught up on sleep.

As we were hanging out that afternoon I noticed a Piper Cub flying lazily overhead. These planes were often around providing some level of observation for various service units so I didn't think much of it. At least, I didn't think much of it until it tilted toward us and fired a little projectile our way.

Red smoke began emerging from the trees right across the canal from us.

Nardelli and I were practitioners of the fine art of fire missions so it was pretty clear to us that red smoke meant someone was marking this area for some sort of friendly fire. That could be a hundred types of bad. Helicopter gunships, artillery, air strikes, you name 'em.

I got on the radio to our battalion headquarters and asked if this was a mistake. Did they spot us and think we were the enemy? They said wait.

A minute later we got this.

"The Air Force has a bombing run on that smoke coming up in...ahhh...just under two minutes now"

I looked up the canal and sure enough off in the distance I could see a jet slowly turning to point its nose straight at us.

"Call them off," I yelled into the radio. We all sounded the alarm. "Air Strike! Air Strike! Get away from the canal."

No one needed prompting. Word spread up and down the line instantly. We grabbed our shit and started running as fast as we could.

The battalion radio guy needlessly deadpanned, "You might want to get back from that canal."

Thanks, Sherlock.

This was not an organized withdrawal. We grabbed weapons and packs and just plain high-tailed it as fast as we could to see how far we could get in less than two minutes. The terrain was wooded and brushy but it had decent footing and we made pretty good progress except that damn entrenching tool kept banging against my leg as I ran.

Now, I didn't stop running but I did manage to unhook that shovel and toss it aside.

We had probably made a couple hundred yards by the time the bomb went off. There was only one before the mission was scrapped. Indeed it had been the observation plane pilot thinking he had spotted an infestation of Viet Cong rather than American soldiers getting a few hours of lounging about. Good thing for him it was a big country and he would never meet us face to face.

So we wandered back to our original spots intending to hang out as long as we could before someone made us get back to humping through the rice paddies, humping being the verb associated with packing heavy gear on long marches.

Once we settled in I got a nice visit from the sergeant whose picture you see above. He had a huge jackpot winner grin on his face.

"Lord," he said. "In our hasty retreat it appears you might have misplaced this."

In his hand was that damn shovel.

*January 25, 1968*
*Dear Mom,*

*No real news today but I thought I'd write to you anyway. I must admit that after you've been gone about as long as I have , the novelty of writing to a G.I. wears off and for that reason my mail continues to diminish as the days go on.*

*One good thing I may not have told you before — my R & R begins February 27 in Australia. I am really looking forward to it but I hate to think of how it will be to come back to this mess after being there.*

*I'm enclosing a picture that was taken of me sometime just after New Year's. In this particular flick I'm much drier than usual. I'm going to use it for the cover photo for my forthcoming novel "How I Won the War with a Long Antenna."*

*Please send care packages as I am continuing to grow skinnier as time goes on.*

*Well before I sound all too depressed, I'll end this one here and write again and try to sound more cheerful.*

*Your Son,*
*Wilhelm I*

# 20

# HUMAN GPS

HERE IS A STRANGE EPIPHANY that popped into my head as I was writing all this.

Shockingly, I have "A-Type" blood somewhere in my veins. Not Type A as in blood type. Rather, "A Type" as in I can be organized, rigid, and structured. I can be a detail guy. I can be a predictable, on time, on target reliable guy. It didn't last long but that was me in Vietnam.

This little self-revelation has me laughing because I just never thought about it this way before. All through school my report cards and essays came back saying "Sloppy Work." As a young reporter I cultivated notes that were all but unreadable. As a manager I refused to have a schedule, preferring brief hallway or open door office encounters. I didn't want people to talk about stuff, I wanted them to do stuff. Heck, for a number of years I ran a $100 million a year multi-platform broadcast operation in apparent chaos because that's what worked

Here's one of the company commanders who trusted me with the detail work.

for me. I was agile, decisive, fast and competitive. I think I had an uncanny knack for prioritizing which problems needed immediate attention and which could be flat out ignored.

One time many years ago someone charged breathlessly into my office and demanded that I come quickly, the sports guys were having a big shouting match and it might come to blows. You should have seen the look on his face when I shrugged and said let me know if someone gets hurt. Sports guys fighting would never be a priority. Faltering on a lead story would be a priority. A client threatening to move their money to cable would be a priority. TV sports guys fighting? Come on.

Sometimes I drove people a little crazy. My informal style was a risky strategy but in my view a successful strategy. It was also so much more fun than being a reliable stooge. Who wants to be that guy, right?

Well, in Vietnam I was exactly that guy. I was that reliable stooge. My life depended on it. My friends' lives depended on it. I left nothing to chance. Once I realized this war had nothing to do with the North versus the South and that my company was chasing indigenous rebels around in their own rice paddies, I knew we couldn't really win anything. There would always be rice farmers, they would always be Viet Cong friendly and they would simply outlast us. As stated, my only mission became survival. I went at it with a vengeance.

Prior to our field missions the company commanders all went to some high level meeting where they learned the battle plan for lack of a better term. They were given coordinates for check points and objectives and all the locations where we would be dropped in either by boat or by chopper. There were sweeps and blocking positions and all types of that big dick military jargon. But in the end it all came down to map work and the Army had fantastically detailed maps that laid out the entire landscape. That was where I came in.

I have loved maps all my life probably starting with hikes through the Cascades when I was a kid. These Army maps were beautiful creations. I was enthralled by the markings of every little clump of trees and that, combined with my survival attitude, led me to work those maps. My then company commander had little patience for pinpointing all the objectives so he turned the battle plans over to me the night before each mission. I marked all the co-ordinates. I studied the various features of every place we might go. I looked for danger zones. I intended to know my exact longitude and latitude at every minute of every day. Long before I ever heard the term GPS I was a human GPS. I could tell you within a meter where we were almost all of the time.

Nardelli was the artillery guy so he had to know these things too. We compared notes constantly because one of us would be directing artillery fire or air strikes. It seems quite odd in retrospect that punk draftee kids had this kind of responsibility but the fact is we did. I would be home and out of the Army and still be too young to legally buy a drink. But out here we had stepped up. We knew what we were doing. We had a big stake in all this. People trusted us to do it right.

Nardelli and I even argued about the Army's arcane way of directing artillery fire missions. The Army way which Nardelli learned in artillery school was to figure out where you were and then tell the battery from that point go north 250 meters and then east 250 meters to hit the target. That seemed so dumb to me. If you know where you are why do it in two steps? Tell them to simple go NE (Shoot an azimuth of 45 degrees) for 300 yards and blow it up. We argued about it all the time and never did get an answer. But the overriding fact here is we studied this stuff conscientiously to make sure we controlled things effectively. You get it, right? We were A-Types and didn't even know it.

I also hate to admit this because it's something else I never considered until I started this writing and remembering things. There was something weirdly satisfying about seeing an F-4 Phantom fly in low and put a napalm canister on the exact spot you asked for it. I apologize if I sound like a heartless Robert Duvall in Apocalypse Now. His character coined the phrase "I love smell of napalm in the morning." In my world it was so much more about seeing evidence of control in the midst of total mayhem.

We did another thing a couple of times that might have been questionable but I would probably do again. Sometimes we would be engaged in what we would call back then a "dust up." It would be longish range stuff that would probably end without casualties. Both sides pretty much knew where the other was and if everyone stayed put it would peter out and end. But sometimes that Delta Devil Six guy in the chopper would want us to pursue Chuck and company into areas where they were in bunkers and where we would risk serious casualties. It was at times like this I occasionally invited one of the machine gunners to sit next to me and unleash a torrent of fire while I explained over the radio to the colonel we were under heavy fire, were fully engaged and unable to get into positon to do whatever silly thing he had in mind. An M-60 machine gun is a noisy bastard.

The colonel in the helicopter was a slave to different goals than ours. He had to write dispatches and after action reports. Body counts were huge to him in those days and he was expected to produce. From his perspective it was a reasonable military action to pursue the enemy. To us it was too much risk for whatever reward might be out there.

This is probably a good place to point out that even though I hated the Army I did not hate the people in the Army. I never met anyone who was reckless with our lives. There were extraordinary people in the Army including in all likelihood this colonel. He was probably a high achieving West Point graduate who had dedicated his life to military service. If it were practical he would have been down with us in the mud charging after the Viet Cong. But our perspectives were vastly different at that point. He was still trying to win a war. We just wanted to live.

People who know me will be surprised by that I've just written. I have lived my life at various times as a risk-taker. I drove fast cars and motorcycles. I covered wars in the Middle East for three years. I have never respected authority.

I always described myself as an idea guy to make sure no one expected me to do the paperwork. I was a leader but largely in the sense of hiring really good people, turning them loose and hoping for the best. I can be easily distracted by any shiny object. I have the attention span of a gnat. But am I really like this or did I just slide into this because I relaxed after surviving Vietnam.

Good question. All I can say is that when my life depended on it everything went under the microscope. Later in life I called people who were like what I was in Vietnam detail-oriented buzz killers. Sorry.

# 21

# MORE ON THE COLONEL AND VC BODY COUNTS

SPEAKING OF VIET CONG BODY counts in Vietnam, they were 100% wrong 100% of the time. If body counts were accurate someone would be fired for incompetence. Please disregard every single news report you read about Vietnam from 1963 to 1975. If the term enemy body count appeared anywhere it was exaggerated. It was distorted and blown so far out of proportion that Pinocchio would have been embarrassed.

I swear this following story is true to the very best of my recollection. We were out in the boonies one day and received some small arms fire from a tree line a few hundred yards to our left. It didn't sound like much but Nardelli called in a fire mission to blow up the tree line. That was always safer than actually hiking over there and getting into a serious fire fight. The artillery he called in was efficient. He reduced that little plot of land to rubble. Even the red ants were looking for a new zip code. And all I got was a colonel on the radio demanding to know the body count.

My company commander loved watching me squirm through these conversations which he should have been having himself. The damn colonel was his boss, not mine. But he just stood back and watched me wiggle. We really only had two choices. We could send a team of people across dangerous open territory to root around in shell craters for body parts or I could make up a plausible lie and take a long smoke break. So I put on my Plausible Liar hat and went for it. The following is a pretty good account of what was actually said over the radio. I told him we killed three Viet Cong.

"You only got three?" the colonel asked.

I didn't want to disappoint him so I embellished.

"Well, that's three confirmed. There might have been five of six 'probables' too." A probable was a moronic statistic where you counted up how many VC you think you might have killed. It was far less credible than a wild ass guess.

"So about ten, then," the colonel replied.

"Yes, sir. Three plus five or six is right about ten."

I should argue? Remember, at this point I only had one goal. I was working to get myself and my guys home safely.

"Okay," the colonel concluded. "I'll call it in as a dozen. You okay with that?"

"Affirmative," I said.

It was a subtle exchange but what that meant was that if anyone ever asked would I back him up. Of course I would.

In point of fact the original three were mythical. We really had no idea. It looked pretty bad out there but they could have escaped. It's still a mystery. We stayed safe and the colonel got his body count. Everybody wins. But that's not the end of this story.

A few days later we were back in basecamp and one of the guys brought over a copy of the Army newspaper the Stars and Stripes. The main headline read "120 Viet Cong Killed in Raging Delta Battle." We went on to read that it was our battalion that did all this killing. The guys were all mystified. And then it hit me.

"Oh yeah, I told that colonel we killed three VC a few days ago in that little dustup in the tree line."

I can only imagine what happened after that. The Battalion must have lied to the Brigade, the Brigade must have lied even more to the Division, probable kills became confirmed kills and by the time this chicken fried nonsense got to the press office at MACV Headquarters in Saigon we had sliced through the Delta like a hot knife through butter. The Stars and Stripes made us sound like heroes. In fact, there had been no battle.

I have used this little story over the years to teach certain employees how to be subversive if that's what it takes to get the job done right. A good subversive never tells people in advance what they are going to do. And they never ask for permission. If I asked my company commander that day for permission to lie to the colonel he might have said no since it would become his lie instead of mine. A true subversive undermines authority by simply doing the right thing without warning and then lets the bosses deal with it. That day, my boss was one of the people I was keeping safe. He didn't say a word. But I did get a smile and a hearty thumbs-up.

> *January 29, 1968*
> *Dear Mom,*
>
> *It is now about four-thirty in the morning and since we have our company spread out all around our base camp perimeter all I have to do is sit here in our orderly room and answer radios. This is one of the benefits of being a radio man — you get out of a little work sometimes.*
>
> *By way of trickery, politics and sheer luck I will be leaving on R & R for Sydney, Australia on the 26th of February. Needless to say I am looking forward to it. The thought of walking down a street full of round-eye women speaking English seems absolutely unbelievable but if I try very, very hard I will be able to adjust to it. By the time I get back I will be half-way through with my little stint in Viet Nam.*

[Note: I obviously was not keeping track of whom I had told what since I seem to have announced my R&R assignment in consecutive letters. My poor memory has continued to bounce downhill since 1968 at an alarming rate.]

*We have finally figured out why we are in Viet Nam. This is really not a war but a mass program of realistic training so we will have the best possible preparation for the next Korean War which should be scaled up just after the next Presidential fiasco in November.*

[Note: 2017 Bill says "huh?"]

*So what's the story on the move north? I still think you should buy a house in the U District so I could walk to school (I still have to conduct a few discussions with our State Motor Vehicle Dept. to get my license back).*

*Tomorrow we go out to a place called Vinh Kim about 3 kilometers from here and we'll be staying out for the Lunar New Year's holiday that should be mass confusion. It's fun because we just set up in a village and don't move for three days and we wander around the market place and buy junk off the locals.*

*My pen has just dried so I'll sign off.*

*Take it easy and don't forget to send goodies. (How about some Jiffy Pop popcorn?)*

*Son # 1*

[Note: This last letter is notable in that we really did think we were in for a three day lark in Vinh Kim. It was rotating assignment we got every month or two and it was a pleasant (if anything could be pleasant) break from our normal missions. These people were used to having troops in their village and were very friendly. They may have known the Tet Offensive was about to turn our world upside down, but we didn't. We were looking at some gravy (easy duty), a truce and that R&R down the road.]

# 22

# TET

OUR INTRODUCTION TO TET TOOK place just after that last letter was written. We set up a security detail in the little hamlet of Vinh Kim. It was located outside the western boundary Dong Tam, our base camp on the Mekong River. The Viet Cong liked to fire mortars from the general area to harass the basecamp so the various units traded off coming out here to discourage them. It was considered light duty.

The people were friendly and always wanted to trade the usual Coke for C-Rations which was fine with us. But that night we got a hint that Tet may not be the happy ceasefire we had been expecting.

An intelligence report was passed on not long after we arrived suggesting a North Vietnamese Army battalion was just across the little Mekong tributary the town was built on. Beyond that there were reports of locals gathering up containers of gasoline for the NVA who it was believed wanted to burn the town. Remember, we had no big picture at this point. We just had un- fathomable information smacking us in the head.

MP's defend the U.S. Embassy in Saigon alongside their dead fellow soldiers during the early hours of the Tet Offensive. (Associated Press)

We went from light duty to holy shit in two

sentences. The NVA had never been within two hundred miles of this place before. Four hundred uniformed enemy soldiers across a stream they might be able to wade across was scary stuff. There were only about thirty of us here in town with another fifty or sixty guys spread out over a mile wide circle. Believe me we got busy in a hurry.

We reset our perimeter, laid out claymore mines, put out listening posts and anything else we could think of. We didn't want to be hanging out in a burning town.

It was a very long night and I was awake for much of it making sure our perimeter people stayed awake. Maybe they failed to grasp this danger. I don't know. I never could figure out why the threat of waking up covered in gasoline would not have kept guards a little more alert but it didn't. I think at various times that night I had to wake up four or five guys.

By dawn we did start to get the big picture. There was a nation-wide offensive that had been launched all across South Vietnam. We didn't hear what happened with that NVA battalion but we think it bypassed us to overrun the provincial capital of My Tho a couple of miles away. It was clear our light little security assignment was obviously over. We had swapped comfort for chaos in very short order.

We were on helicopters early and by mid-morning we were in the Saigon suburb of Cholon where the Viet Cong had among other things captured the horse racing track. The fact that a unit from the Delta went to the Saigon area was a clear indication of the level of concern these attacks had caused. Smoke rising over the capital did not make anyone feel very secure that morning.

This wasn't just chaos for the American command. This was pure panic for them in those first hours.

We were only involved in light fighting in Cholon that day but for the better part of the next ten days we would be on the move.

The day after Cholon we were back in the Delta going street by street through My Tho where the NVA had tried to dig in. We had used a great deal of artillery fire to move them out but many not as much as what happened in the days to come. At one point we were relatively close to a Delta town called Ben Tre when an unnamed officer offered one of the lasting quotes of the entire Vietnam conflict.

The officer told AP Correspondent Peter Arnett his rationale for shelling and bombing the town and its civilian population to rout out the Viet Cong.

"It became necessary to destroy the town to save it."

There was a lot of that during Tet and that quote got plenty of play back home. We did blow up a lot of towns to drive out the Viet Cong. We did inflict serious casualties to the Viet Cong. There really were also quite a few civilian casualties. This was not the out in the open fighting we were accustomed to expect. We were in urban areas. Residents either fled or got caught in the crossfire. There was little time for making any distinctions.

We were told over and over what a great job we had done defeating the Viet Cong. The Tet Offensive was a complete military failure for the North Vietnamese and Viet Cong according to the army brass. And who believed that? Nobody.

This "failing" enemy had just proved it could strike at any place and any time. Never mind most of them were driven back at great cost. What Americans saw on TV was their soldiers fighting in the American Embassy, clearing our main air bases in Saigon and fighting a room by room battle in the northern city of Hue. These things just weren't supposed to happen and no comparisons of body counts would make these images any less horrifying.

The enemy took a calculated risk in terms of sacrificing a large number of troops to win a public relations campaign in the U.S. That goal was achieved. Tet was the ultimate tipping point for American public opinion. It didn't end the war. It didn't stop the bombing. But it did turn the tide.

*February 3, 1968*

*Dear Mom —*

*Happy Lunar New Year. You wouldn't believe what's been going on here. They have actually convinced me there is a war going on. We are hoping it's reached its peak and will start settling down to normal around here but one never knows. I don't know what you've gotten in the papers but somebody is definitely having a hell raising party in South Viet Nam.*

*So far I've been lucky (how long can luck hold out) and been spared most of the action but a little is bad enough. I am suffering from a severe case of "yellow fever" which means I'm getting a little bit nervous about the whole situation.*

*We've been out playing for the last four days and now we're back in Dong Tam waiting to get our regular ration of mortars. I'm not trying to scare you but at least give you a little idea. I'm all right so far and as long as we don't celebrate TET every day I should make it all right.*

[Note: Tet was a huge escalation for us in terms of both fighting intensity and just plain difficult work. We really did not get much of a break for the first four or five days. If I sound a little rattled in this letter, I was.]

*My main problem is lack of sleep and half the reason I don't sleep is I'm too tired and too tense. I think I've aged about ten more years in the last week.*

*I hope you get this letter soon so you'll know I'm all right. We've been having trouble with mail since all flights are priority.*

*By the time you get this I might even be in Australia, never to be heard from again. I could live easily without seeing this goofy place again.*

*Who knows, maybe the war will end tomorrow. No luck, you watch, next week they'll be raising hell along the DMZ.*

*Well, what?*

*Your cheerful Son,*
*Bill*

# 23

# FEET

JUST ABOUT EVERY GRUNT IN our unit suffered from a condition known as immersion foot or as I learned later reading about it, "paddy foot." Our feet were just plain wet for days at a time and at some point entire units had to be taken out of the field and ordered to go shoeless for several days to allow for healing. The skin on our feet would be soaked to the point it would simply start to peel off chaffing in our socks and our feet would completely scab over. Our red feet reminded me of seeing salmon spawning when I was a kid growing up in the Northwest. Swimming upstream and bouncing off rocks for hundred miles or more removed most of their scales leaving them with a sickly red appearance. That's what our feet looked like. They looked like big red hunks of raw meat. It scared the heck out of the sailors who saw them but in fact it wasn't too painful. This looked bad and needed to be addressed but was really

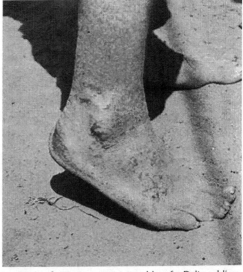

Immersion foot was a constant problem for Delta soldiers.

nothing compared to the related trench foot soldiers experienced in World War I. That added frostbite to the equation and in some cases actually required amputation.

# 24

# NARDELLI

BOB NARDELLI WAS KILLED ON February 9, 1968.

Bob and a dozen or so other soldiers were on a patrol just outside the north perimeter of the 9th Infantry Division base camp at Dong Tam. We had just completed that ten day series of exhausting missions taking back Delta towns and territory overrun by the Viet Cong in the Tet Offensive.

We arrived in base camp as weary as we had ever been. There was a lull in the fighting. We were told to rest. Most of us did.

Someone decided it was prudent that day to work a light patrol around our base camp. It was less than three miles of walking since the Mekong River provided the longest border. In a military sense this is what we would call a "cakewalk." The danger was extremely minimal. Daylight enemy activity was almost unheard of around our perimeter.

Bob was always the active one. He volunteered to go along. We didn't even know he was out there. My guess is that he just thought it would be a good way to pass the

My friend and our artillery forward observer Bob Nardelli.

time. We all had that little clock in our heads pointing to the date
far off in the future when we would "rotate" as it was called and
catch that plane home. Maybe this little cakewalk would make his
clock tick a little faster.

Internet photo depicting a scene similar to the one that left Bob Nardelli dead. In Bob's
case he had handed the rifle up to the other soldier butt first. (Pinterest)

Bob's death was a horrible, nightmarish accident. He was shot in
the chest at close range with his own rifle. The picture above gives
you some idea of what the scene must have looked like. As soldiers
waded through muddy canals it was often easiest to have someone
help pull them out. It was not at all uncommon for one soldier to
hold out his rifle and create better leverage to for the person pulling
from above. It happened countless times every day.

This case was different for two dreadful mistakes that happened
one after the other. First, Bob's M-16 was loaded as would have been
standard but somehow the safety was not engaged. There are vets
who might say this was okay but I would argue to have the safety
engaged to avoid accidental firing. That certainly was the norm

to me and my fellow soldiers at the time. The second mistake is not arguable. The soldier helping Bob out of the mud apparently reached down and inadvertently pulled the trigger as he tried to help Bob out of the mud. We have no specific information about how that happened. It was wet and muddy. His hand could have slipped. He might have lost his footing. There is an endless list of possibilities all with the same result. The trigger was pulled and Bob took a bullet at point blank range.

I don't know how the word travelled so quickly but we knew all the details of this incident within minutes. Bob did not die instantly. A Medevac helicopter was sent even though he was less than a half a mile away. Several of us ran to the base hospital in time to see it land. When the stretcher came out of the chopper we got yet another shocking Vietnam image seared into our memories. Bob's chest was awash in the brightest color of scarlet blood I had ever seen. It appeared phosphorescent even in bright sunlight. The medics lowered the stretcher on to a cart and then walked the cart into the emergency entrance. That walk was ominous. They came back in just minutes to tell us that Bob didn't make it.

I can only speak for myself on this but I don't think guys spend a lot of time talking about friendship. Certainly Bob and I were way too casual to put words to what was a pretty obvious close friendship. We had shared the most intense experiences of our lives for several months sometimes for days on end. As the radio operators there were many practical reasons for us to be together. There was even a tactical reason. Everybody in the infantry has a buddy. He was mine. We had each other's back by military design and as a matter of personal commitment. He was like a wise-cracking little brother. I was the older, wiser 20 year-old. I can't recall even ever arguing with the guy. He was always in too good of a mood. There were many unspoken bonds in Vietnam and I suspect personal friendships were among them.

The Tet offensive and Bob's death were both pivotal but for different reasons. We were smothered with propaganda that we had dealt the Viet Cong a death blow during Tet. At the same time America was coming to the same conclusion many of us had already reached. The war was unwinnable and probably unjust. The image of Viet Cong on the grounds of the American Embassy in Saigon had vastly more influence on the country than all the hyped up body counts that followed. When Walter Cronkite had had enough, the rest of the country was not far behind.

For me personally Bob's death was a sort of emotional tipping point. I had seen death and destruction up until now but this was very personal. We were the guys who were careful. Survival was our priority. Details were our currency. Yet here he was killed in this most careless accident that repudiated everything we had worked to accomplish.

There was no dramatic moment where I went cold on the world but this was the start of an emotional shutdown that I think lasted for many years and possibly decades. Things like this don't have exact beginnings or ends. It was very slow and partial shutdown. In retrospect I liken it to invisible fingers steadily squeezing vulnerabilities out of my life. I know this sounds self-centered and indulgent but I think it affected my relationships with people for a long time. When I got back to college most of my friends were people from high school. When I found a profession it allowed me to share intense moments with the people we filmed for news stories but I was always the detached observer. I moved a lot. I didn't engage in the most obvious of social situations. I didn't get married until I was forty. Maybe this all would have happened without Vietnam but there is no real way to tell. Honestly, I don't think it was until I got married and we had four children that the protective shell I had built around myself finally crumbled.

It's very hard to define how Vietnam in general or Bob's death in particular fueled all this but I have to suspect there was some connection between all these experiences and what I would call an emotional reserve. A guy at work many decades ago described me as having the face of a choir boy and the heart of a cobra. It was a clever line. It also stung a little because it was not totally off the mark. I was cool under pressure sometimes to a fault. I sometimes was professional to a fault. Later, after I was married and settled down I became a much more open and caring person and a vastly more humane leader of the people who worked for me.

It was literally nearly twenty years before I told anyone about Bob and the nature of his death. It was one of the countless things buried about the whole war experience. The first person I told about Bob was a female friend after a few drinks at dinner one night. It was kind of a shell-breaking moment for me. She obviously did not notice this was a big deal for me.

Her response was, "That's awful. Are we going to have dessert?"

Later, when my kids got older and we visited the Vietnam Memorial the whole story came out, old pictures came out and Bob became a known figure in our family. One of my daughters made this rubbing of his name on the Wall.

Another daughter sang the Dixie Chicks "Travelin' Soldier" in a talent competition. It was a favorite of mine not just as an evocative reminiscence of Vietnam but it reminded me of Bob Nardelli in particular. In the song a young soldier meets a waitress who agrees to write letters to him while he serves in the army. They become close. He goes to war. The rest is fairly predictable. Over the years Bob sort of morphed into that soldier in the song to me. Like so many others he had that "sort of" girlfriend who wrote regularly even if it wasn't a formal or committed relationship. I always thought of her as the piccolo player in this, the last verse.

> *One Friday night at a football game*
> *The Lord's Prayer said and the Anthem sang*
> *A man said, "Folks would you bow your heads*
> *For a list of local Vietnam dead."*
> *Crying all alone under the stands*
> *Was a piccolo player in the marching band*
> *And one name read but nobody really cared*
> *But a pretty little girl with a bow in her hair*

It's a beautiful song performed with what I consider magical sweetness by Natalie Mains of the Dixie Chicks (and my daughter at that contest). But even that song didn't address one key question. Why had I never contacted Bob's family? We lived in LA for nearly three years back in the 90's. We drove through Redondo Beach. I even looked in the phone book once and found names that must have been related. But I just couldn't make myself do it. I wish I could tell you why. I knew it was the right thing to do but I held back for some reason.

Now fast forward to about 2012 when I was reading a novel called "Second Watch" by J.A. Jance. Jance is a Seattle-based writer who is best known for her smart and highly localized series of novels about a Seattle homicide detective. My reporter wife had done stories with Jance and I had actually met her at a neighbor's house one time at a book party.

In the novel Jance appropriated people she had known from high school who had been involved in Vietnam and wrote them into the story lines of the book. In effect, she fictionalized real people. Then at the end of the book she wrote an extremely compelling case asking readers to look back for the loose ends in their lives attached to the Vietnam War and to reach out to those who still may be suffering. It was a little eerie reading that author's note because it felt as though she was writing directly to me. She was telling me to get off my butt. She lit a fire that I had not been able to light myself.

My wife went to work on this and learned pretty quickly that Bob's mother and father had died some years back. In those conversations she learned of a stepmother who seemed hard to reach and when we did finally reach her it was not a huge success. She was suspicious and even a little hostile. Surprise phone calls forty some years late are not always appreciated.

The army had apparently not told Bob's family the details of his death. That didn't help either. We didn't make much progress with the stepmother but we learned that he had a younger sister who lived in North Carolina and through a series of negotiations the stepmother sent our email address to her. That was when we finally reached our goal.

Bob's sister had been five years-old at the time of his death and she remembered very little about him. She had no picture other than a high school annual photo. The family did not discuss him very much so she knew very little of what he was like and what kind of a person he had become. We were able to fill in many of those blanks by phone and email and I found several pictures I sent her. Our contact was a little shocking to her but she obviously appreciated the effort we had made and she was totally forgiving of me for taking so long to do something so simple and obvious. This was the completion of a torturous circle but with thanks to J.A. Jance, my wife and Bob's sister my extremely tardy obligation was completed.

Bob was just a month shy of his 19th birthday when he died.

*February 15, 1968*

*Dong Tam*
*Dear Mom,*

*Well, the Valentine's Day checkpoint has come and gone and the halfway mark is next on the grid. Presently we are on a 24 hour stand-by to pack up and move — yes everything — South, which has up to now been sort of un-conquered by Americans. We'll be the first large American unit in the area and from what sketchy information I can obtain we'll be based at a place called Can Tho (sp?) which is on the southern tip of South Vietnam and all the way into unknowns of the Delta.*

*This all sounds rather poor but it really always sounds worse than it is. We'll be living on the ships again which will be a vast relief from the dust, dirt and incoming mortar rounds at our Dong Tam base camp.*

*By the way, what did Tom Mead ever do about this Army business? I'd like you to give him my address if you could so I could give him some information that is rather shrouded at Basic Training Camps about the country.*

*So where's the goodies? Popcorn, cashews, food and any-thing else I've asked for so far. Also I want a copy of* Atlas Shrugged *by Ayn Rand and I've had no luck getting it so far. I've read just about all the rest of her stuff so if you could find this one I'd like it.*

*It's been a bad week for my friends around here. About a week ago an artillery forward observer that's been with us quite a while and slept next to me when we were in garrison was shot and killed with his own weapon while climbing out of an irrigation ditch on a patrol just outside Dong Tam. Two days later they exploded a mine and fragments broke Scotty's arm and cut his ear. I don't know if I've mentioned him or not but he's been one of the best friends I've made over here. He's in Saigon now and we're hoping he gets sent home. This is the second time he's been hit and he's 24 years old with a wife and two kids and really had no business over here anyway.*

[Note: This letter is astounding to me for several reasons. First of all, as we say in journalism, I buried the lede. I was trying to write a breezy, chatty letter about Valentine's Day, Australia, *Atlas Shrugged* and the like. In the middle of all this I slip in the news about my two close friends, one dead and the other seriously wounded. It seems really callous in retrospect although at the time I may have had some rationale for how I wrote this news. I honestly don't know what I was thinking. Was I protecting my mom or myself? It could very well be that I was just hurting and apparently not yet able to deal with it in any sharable way. I still couldn't give you an answer to what I was thinking although I can assure you these things were quite heavy on my mind at that time and for that matter, even today.]

*I'm still scratchless and still plodding along. You mentioned the antennae and don't worry I don't use that big one very often. The usual one is only about 3 feet long.*

*Australia is getting closer and closer — only 11 days and I'll be a beach bum in Sydney with a blonde and a sports car. My intentions are, of course, strictly honorable, as is the case of all G.I.'s on R & R.*

*I've been slow in writing Kathy because I lost her address but today when I was sorting my stuff and packing I found it and I'll write her soon.*

*Other than that, not much new. Be sure and write and send some junk. Even cookies. I'm getting skinnier by the day.*

*Your Son,*
*Stokley Carmichael Jr.*

# 25

# LEARNING TO OPPOSE THE WAR IN SIX EASY LESSONS

I can't say I was a rabid supporter of the Vietnam War when I went into the Army but early on I thought we were doing the right thing. To be honest I was mostly aware of it in terms of how it would affect me. I was probably not sophisticated enough to consider it from any other point of view. Certainly there was an anti-war movement in 1966 but it was in its infancy compared to what it would later become.

There were a few concepts obviously at work on me. We had been programmed all our lives to fight communism. This seemed to fit that concept. The notion of NORTH Vietnam invading SOUTH Vietnam seemed very much like a war of aggression. This,

too seemed reasonable. I don't recall a thing about the Gulf of Tonkin Incident but I'm reasonably sure it had not been discredited by 1966.

To some degree I bought into all these things. The so-called Domino Theory seemed to make sense. Red China as it was known in those days was the boogeyman supporting movements in Korea, Vietnam, Cambodia and Laos. In many ways it was all very persuasive. I was clearly persuaded early on. The aggression had to be stopped, right? And who could do it? We could, America, the world's righteous traffic cop, of course. A lot of people saw it that way.

Once I arrived in Vietnam I was better able to assess facts and separate them from myths. I was able to note that each country was unique. Labels were not always correct. Motivations were much more complicated than I had believed. Seeing situations up close and on the ground shed a great deal more light on the subject than my previous consumption of information on Vietnam. And all these things slowly turned me against the war.

## 1) Geography

This was my first little epiphany. I probably should have known more about this going in but I was immediately struck by the fact we were fighting indigenous rebels. The Viet Cong were not North Vietnamese. They were fighting on their home turf against their own government. In our little corner of Vietnam this wasn't a war of aggression from the North. This was a revolution. We weren't going to push the Viet Cong back north across the border. We were shooting at them in their own backyards. Certainly they supported Ho Chi Minh and the communist government of North Vietnam. But they were also fighting to re-unify a country divided by colonial powers. They were fighting a Saigon government that had been essentially put and kept in power by the United States. So while we were still fighting communists they had multiple motivations for their actions that went beyond communism. None of this changed my mind instantly but it certainly started the process of doubt.

## 2) Control

The Viet Cong controlled the entire countryside in the Delta area where I served. American units and even South Vietnamese Army units were garrisoned and guarded right up to and including those stationed in the relatively safe Saigon area. Many Americans would have argued the V.C. controlled the area though fear and terror. I suspect in some cases that is correct. But whatever the case the Viet Cong managed to produce considerable loyalty among the rural Vietnamese. We could see that in village after village as we worked our way through ground operations. Even when people were friendly they were reserved and we were guarded in our relations with them. Even with the millions of people in Saigon who reputedly supported the South Vietnamese government we were wary. I felt like we didn't really have any real friends in Vietnam and I suspect my fellow soldiers felt the same way. And if the very people you are there to protect may be supporting your enemy that too caused me to start re-examining my own rationale for being here.

## 3. Motivation

This one was a smack in the face. What were people fighting for and how hard were they fighting? There is something of a lesson to be learned here. Forget about labels for a minute and think of this. One side wanted to re-unify the country. The other side wanted American troops to keep them in power. One side had the Viet Cong who were always on the attack. The other side had the South Vietnamese Army, with all the weaponry America could buy, seemingly unable or unwilling to fight. Is that analysis too simple? Maybe. But those were the obvious facts that seemed to present themselves to soldiers on the ground in the Delta. And when I saw the South Vietnamese leaving all the fighting to us, I had to question their level of motivation. If they weren't willing to fight and die for their own country, why should I?

## 4. Opinions Back Home

News reports about Vietnam had a profound effect on how public opinion had really shifted in 1967 and 1968 to a much broader opposition to the war. It became obvious at some point that no one could really articulate our goals in Vietnam any more. And there were huge factors shaping this shift in public opinion. Americans hated seeing the mounting U.S. casualty numbers. Very few communities were spared from losing young men. More and more Americans, including those of us in the field, began to truly ask ourselves about the rampant corruption in the South Vietnamese government. And frankly fewer and fewer Americans cared how we got out of Vietnam, they just wanted us out. "We've Never Lost a War." "We Can't Surrender." "Peace with Honor." These phrases may have gained some traction but they became less and less applicable to the real situation. And when large factions of the American public began to turn on the very soldiers who were fighting the war, things hit rock bottom. We were fighting someone else's civil war and our country to some large extent wanted us to stop. This was hardly motivation for me to continue fighting the war even though I had little choice but to soldier on.

## 5. The Tet Offensive

There is so much that can be said about Tet but I can give you my two cents pretty quickly.

The Tet Offensive did prove the North Vietnamese and Viet Cong could do anything they wanted and the Vietnamese public would do nothing to stop them. The first 24 hours rocked us back on our heels because we frankly were caught off guard. Our response to the Tet Offensive rocked them back. They seemed to have thought this attack would produce a general uprising and that they could hold their gains. They were wrong. They were beaten back, at some considerable cost, in every place they had attacked. So the Tet Offensive was a military disaster for Ho Chi Minh.

But he probably knew that would happen. The military loss didn't matter the slightest bit because it was a master stroke of public relations. The NVA and V.C. took enormous losses but America went into a panic. Americans saw dead MP's on the steps of our embassy. They saw cities overrun. They saw the scared faces of military commanders and political leaders explaining what had happened.

No amount of body count math was ever going to erase those images. The tide was turning faster than ever against the war and frankly it was for us in the field as well. If the whole country of South Vietnam kept this attack secret from its own government, there's a problem. That didn't seem at the time to be all fear and intimidation. It looked a lot like the people had chosen sides. Why am I risking my neck for people who hate me?

## 6. Waiting Us Out

I did not have a crystal ball but as I prepared to leave Vietnam one thing was pretty certain in my mind. Our enemy was willing to sacrifice its own people in large numbers to win an ultimate victory. They had lots of people and all the time in the world. They had successfully helped push American public opinion to the point of massive demonstrations in our streets. We had our own problems with racial tensions in America and we were reeling from the death of Martin Luther King. Our president, Lyndon Johnson, was giving up his office out of sheer frustration figuring out what to do about Vietnam. The enemy strategy was to wait it out. It wasn't a brilliant strategy. It was an obvious one. They could sustain huge losses if necessary. We could not. They were on their home turf. We were not. They had popular support. We did not. They had a vision and a path to success. We had neither. Now let's get personal. Was I right or wrong to make my only real priority getting myself and my fellow soldiers home alive? Should I have been more "Gung Ho?" Tell me. Because by the end I was pretty much devoid of any positive feelings about what might be accomplished in Vietnam.

Going through these six steps progressively during my time in Vietnam certainly put me in the anti-war camp. I could cite moral grounds or any number of other issues but in the end I just felt like we as a country had been hoodwinked. Our motivations were honorable. Our government meant well. Our soldiers did a fine job. We wanted to help stem the tide of aggression and we took huge losses in that effort. But in the end the people who asked for our help were taking advantage of our good will. They wanted us more to protect their own political skins than to protect their country or their people. Nobody likes to be bamboozled but that's what I believe happened to us in Vietnam. So in the end we were left with a sour taste about the war only to be outdone by the sour welcome we received from our own fellow Americans when we got home.

# 26

# R&R IN AUSTRALIA

It was a pretty radical traffic move. The car swerved sharply and skidded to a halt just in front of us as we walked along a Sydney sidewalk. Did my default switch go straight to psycho killers? We were still a little edgy just off the plane from Vietnam and all.

All four doors flew open and people piled out. Were they religious nuts?

"G'day mates, welcome to Australia," the man said.

A quick scan of the faces lowered the threat level. These were plain old everyday nice people. They had stopped to thank us for fighting in Vietnam. The parents were telling their three kids, ages roughly eight through twelve, that we were heroes protecting Australia. It was truly extraordinary. They had just pulled over to the side of the road to say "thank you."

With all the introductions and greetings over we finally asked.

"How did you know we were American soldiers?"

That triggered peals of laughter.

They made us rent suits at the Sydney Airport. We did not wear them very often once we bought jeans.

"Sorry, mates, but nobody in Australia would go outside with those awful buzz cuts," the dad told us.

We laughed too. We had forgotten momentarily we had hamster sidewalls thanks to our army haircuts. We laughed but I made a little note to self to get a baseball cap.

There were no protests here in Sydney where we had just arrived for R and R, Rest and Relaxation, a one week vacation in the middle of our tours in Vietnam. That old domino theory seemed like the real deal here in Australia where Southeast Asia was pretty close to the north. They still remembered Darwin getting bombed in World War II. They had sent soldiers to fight alongside us in Vietnam and they were truly appreciative. It was a stark contrast to what we would later find when we returned to America.

I was travelling with a guy named Gary Snay who I had run into at the R and R transfer station in Saigon. He and I had looked at each other for a moment and realized we had served together the previous year in Berlin. We buddied up for what turned out to be a great adventure. By the time we met that family we had already ditched our rented suits for stiff jeans and brand new t-shirts and we were enjoying our first day of stress free sunshine in months.

We had just checked into the very fancy Menzies Hotel downtown at absurdly low military rates and we were strategizing on job number one. We had to find girls.

I honestly don't recall which one of us thought of this first but as we gazed out our hotel window we saw a long row of office buildings out behind the hotel. A rare moment of pure genius struck like a thunderclap. These office buildings had to have secretaries. We were inspired. We got busy. Somewhere we found construction paper and a magic marker. In what seemed like just a few short minutes we had fashioned a sign. Two Yanks, Call Room 907. We did not say two desperate, horndog losers who have been deprived of female companionship for seven long months but I think that was pretty clearly implied, right?

Our phone never stopped ringing for the entire week.

In fact, even the very stodgy *Sydney Herald* thought it was inventive enough to put us on their front page.

Now before you imagine the worst let me just say this. We were deluged by large numbers of fun loving, kind-hearted young women who were almost too solicitous. Some wanted to take us to coffee. Some wanted drinks. Some wanted to treat us to fancy dinners where they wouldn't let us pick up the check. None of them wanted to dominate all our time because they wanted us to enjoy Australia and our time here. They wanted us to meet as many people as possible. Could it be they were a little too nice?

It was as though an entire country stopped what it was doing to show us every possible kindness and consideration. From Vietnam to Sydney was like stepping into a new dimension we could never have imagined. We were warmly embraced from start to finish. Those warm feelings of that visit have never worn off.

We were guests on a ferry ride to Manly Beach where they talked me into ordering some type of huge fish at a seafood house. I had no idea where to begin when this monster whole fish arrived staring at me from a large platter. Then we were off to a shark aquarium where we could get a close up look at a hammerhead shark. Somewhere along the way we acquired bathing suits for day trip to Bondi Beach. My letters home indicated we saw kangaroos but I honestly don't remember any of them.

As the week went along we did sort of pair off with a couple of young women who helped us soak up the town. The whole experience was very civilized. Gary and I sometimes exchanged looks but I don't think we really discussed it much. I had never been treated this well in my life. We were having the best times of our lives despite the fact the clock kept counting down inexorably to our departure back to Vietnam.

At one point these ever so nice girls even took us to a strip show. I was a little naïve but what the heck. Strip show, you bet. All these ladies on the stage were stripping down to little pasties and dancing wildly to rock music. It looked pretty good to me after all these months of isolation. There was one older woman near us cheering them on wildly and we were told she was the mom of one of the dancers. That seemed a little weird to me but not as weird as what was coming. At the big finale the dancers all took their bows and then one of them unhooked something and took off her boobs. What? I experienced a brief moment of stunned disbelief. Then I was a little embarrassed. These were all guys dressed up as female strippers. The mom was cheering for her son. Our hosts could not contain their amusement. They couldn't believe I didn't know all along.

"You really didn't know," they laughed.

I guess these guys must have been pretty good.

"I didn't," I replied sheepishly.

We stayed up all night before our morning flight back to the war. We didn't want to give up a single moment of our experience in Australia. All my life I have talked about the great people there. I still think it might be the coolest place on earth populated by the best people on earth. I remember I had to turn down an Australian soldier who wanted to trade me his awesome slouch hat for the stupid little cap we wore with our uniforms. It would have been like trading an Audi for a tricycle. But that's just how the Aussies were. They would give you anything. They were fabulous people and fabulous hosts.

In 2010 I took my family to Australia to see all those old places again. It is still our favorite vacation ever. We were there over the Christmas holidays and the streets were teeming with people. We went to the Opera House, Bondi, Manly and even walked through the old Menzies Hotel. We skipped the dancing drag queens although I did confess to my kids how dumb I had been.

What I recall about the family trip is that with all these thousands of people wandering the streets at the holidays we never saw a police officer the whole time we were there. We were simply surrounded by upbeat, friendly and considerate people and that's how I will always remember this great country.

And in a very belated way Australia, thank you very much. You lifted a young soldier out of his misery and showed him a week that he still cherishes even after these long fifty years. I'll be back again now that I'm retired.

*March 7, 1968*
*Dear Mom,*

No doubt you'll be glad to hear that I've successfully completed my trip to Sydney and I'm safely "home" back in Viet Nam. I haven't gone as far as to return to my unit yet figuring I may just as well fool around for a few days before I return to the drudgery.

Sydney was probably the most event-filled single week of my life and I really can't begin to describe what a good time I had there.

I think the single most outstanding thing was the way everyone there was so eager to go out of their way to make everything perfect. It's the only time in my military "career" where anyone has really appreciated me for anything more than the dollar in my pocket.

The girl I ended up spending the last four days with was from England and she owned an M.G. which made things quite nice and we had a real fine time out at the night spots.

I spent about $200 which is pretty cheap when you consider guys spend sometimes six or seven hundred in Hong Kong or something and spend their whole time with a prostitute. I couldn't quite see that and I'm not at all sorry I went to Sydney. My problem now is arranging to get back which will be a good trick if I can pull it off.

[Note: This was a mindless generalization on my part. I really don't know what guys did at other R&R locations and it is unfair to suggest what I suggested here.]

*I bought zero souvenirs and the only kangaroos I saw were in the Sydney zoo but I did see a couple of real live sharks (from a nice safe ferry boat).*

*It was nice to have a bed and bathtub and I lived like a complete king in my hotel. Breakfast in bed every day (at noon) of course.*

*The girl my friend from Berlin, Gary, was with was the flatmate of mine so everything worked out smoothly.*

*I can sum the whole thing up in one sentence but for your benefit, I'll spare you.*

*Your Son the Traveler,*
*Bill*

# 27

# SURPRISES

VIETNAM WAS FILLED WITH DRUDGERY for American soldiers but every now and then there was a little surprise to break the monotony. And I'm not talking about an ambush breaking the monotony of humping your gear through the boonies. That's more than just a surprise, that's more like total loss of sphincter control. No, what I'm talking about are just little eye openers to tell you the world might still be paying attention.

When I talk about drudgery nothing can be worse than filling sandbags. We spent a day or two at Dong Tam our basecamp sometimes to rest up between field missions. That sounded a lot better than the reality. The reality of it was they had us fill sandbags to line all the buildings to protect them from mortar attacks. I guess if the mortar came through the roof and landed on your bed you were a goner but if it landed just outside the building we made you safe. I believe they had us do this so we would beg them for more combat missions. It was terrible work.

One day we were able to beat the sandbag drill and aimlessly wandered around the base. It was

Who is this guy? That's one of the surprises.

hot, dusty and as I recall the base was infested with giant houseflies that day. At some point an older sergeant called us aside and told us to take a look at the guy across the way talking to a small group of soldiers.

Now I have to come clean here. I have a pretty clear memory of this meeting but the best information I can find does not confirm this individual was actually at Dong Tam in late 1967 or early 1968. The picture above from the Stars and Stripes says it was August of 1967 before I arrived. Did I dream this?

Anyway, the sergeant said "That's Omar Bradley."

As in General of the Army Omar Bradley? The guy who commanded all the American forces in Europe in World War II? The guy who helped punch Hitler's ticket? Standing here at Dong Tam? It was indeed. Now that was certainly worth walking over to see what was up.

The most striking thing about him was that he was decidedly unmilitary. He was not a fire and brimstone General. He was actually pretty quiet and asked guys what they were getting from home and if the mail was getting through fast enough. He wore army fatigues but with no insignia of rank or anything else. He was just a very pleasant old fellow shooting the breeze with a bunch of guys. Much later I learned that he had become known in World War II as the G.I.'s general because he treated all the troops with great respect. It was said about him that whenever he issued an order he included the word please. That G.I. general moniker certainly fit what we saw that day.

The crowd got pretty large very quickly and I never actually spoke to him personally but it was still a memorable little accident that beat the heck out of filling sandbags.

Another little surprise I had over there one day wasn't as pleasant but it certainly provided a great deal of entertainment since I was the victim of a little prank. Actually it was a pretty big prank when you think of what the guy did.

We were returning to our base one time on our Tango boats which I have already described as river borne landing craft that took us all through the Delta. They were open boats but with canvas covering all the troops to provide shade. On this particular day I was sleepy and figured with the mission over I could crawl up on top of the awning and take a nap. In fact, I was quite pleased with myself as I stretched out on the warm, comfy canvas and closed my eyes. This was quite pleasant. Or at least, it was for a while.

At some point I awoke from the sunlight going dark for just enough of a blip to send a brain signal that something was amiss. That was followed quickly by a blast of noise so loud that it rattled my very bones beyond all measure. It's still amazing to me how fast the human brain can process information like this and produce some sort of adrenaline/fear reaction. It would be a vast understatement to say I was startled. Let's go with panic stricken.

I then heard a lot of wows and look at that comments from down below and when I did look up I realized what had happened. I had been buzzed by an F-4 Phantom jet. It had come up behind us at extreme speed and shot across my body maybe 20 feet above me. The sun was blotted out before the noise because it was probably going 700mph and the noise had to actually catch up with it. I'm sure there was a Phantom pilot chuckling that day and once I figured it all out I was chuckling too.

Now I didn't usually sleep when I had down time in Vietnam because even in the worst of times I tried to have a book with me. I had always been a reader and reading seemed to pass the time in this place where passing the time was like a pro sport.

I really don't recall how I got books. I'm sure people sent them to me. I'm sure we swapped them among ourselves but a lot of that is gone from my memory banks. What is not gone from my memory is that for a long time I wanted to read the book *Atlas Shrugged* by Ayn Rand. I read her other standard *The Fountainhead* during my stunted year in college and I really loved the sort of one unbending man against the world themes of her stories. I was way too uneducated to realize she was promoting her own brand of conservative self-reliant philosophy. I was just drawn to the monumental struggles her characters faced and overcame.

Let's go back to Dong Tam where I was walking along a path next to a ditch by the airstrip one day. I have no idea what I was doing but I saw what appeared to be a paperback sticking out of the mud on the bank of the ditch. Seeing any book in Vietnam was like finding cold cash on a city sidewalk so I clamored down the bank and dug it out. It was a tattered but still intact copy of *Atlas Shrugged.*

This was such a mind-boggling coincidence that other people might have claimed it was some religious sign. I just thought it was amazing good luck and started the dusting and drying process so I could start reading.

As always, there was a little hitch in the get-along as my Texas friends liked to say. We had to leave on an operation at one in the morning so there would be precious little time for reading. In fact, there was no time for reading for nearly twenty four hours when we finally set up camp in some now forgotten hell hole someplace. I was finally ready to read but the light would soon be failing.

Now, I was a very good radio operator in Vietnam. I was competent and reliable. I was steady. But on this night putting a radio in my hands would prove to be very expensive for the

American taxpayer. That's because as darkness descended on the rice paddies that night I suggested to my far away superiors that we might be hearing enemy activity outside our perimeter.

Perhaps, I suggested helpfully, they might send up some illumination flares to help us see what was going on. Somewhere a few miles away artillery battery fired off an illumination round that was perfectly adequate to allow me to keep reading. After a couple minutes I asked for another. And so on. I believe I maintained the fiction of possible enemy activity for about an hour and a half so I could continue reading *Atlas Shrugged*. I must have finally started falling asleep so at some point I backed off.

I never did add up how many illumination rounds I ordered up that night and I never even guessed at the cost. But really, it was probably just a few thousand bucks here or there in the middle of a big expensive war. I wanted to read my book. Who would ever know? And now that they do know, what can they do? I am reasonably certain the statute of limitations on felonious appropriation of illumination has run out.

So yes, there were some breaks in the drudgery. There were some surprises. And I have to say I managed to make some good memories, particularly when given the opportunity to go rogue.

*March 10, 1968*

*Dear Mom —*

*I got back to my unit today and we are back living on ships, floating about in the big muddy Mekong. I got your packages and everything was just fine. You can rest assured now that your little boy won't starve.*

*Speaking of your little boy, he is now a real live sergeant in the big bad Infantry. It was a little surprise they had for me when I got back. They just didn't know what an integral part I was till I was gone for a while.*

*You mentioned that you didn't know where Dong Tam was so here goes — It is about 40 miles due south of Saigon along the Mekong River. It doesn't usually show on maps but if you see a town called My Tho it's about two miles from us.*

*I'm still on Cloud Nine from Sydney but I guess soon enough the regular depression that comes free with my occupation will set in.*

*You mentioned that I should write a note to your friend Joni but using your usual good eye for the impractical, you didn't mention her address. You can give her mine if you like and she can write me a letter of introduction if she wants to hear from me. Thank her for the cookies too.*

*Meanwhile I am existing with about 178 days left to do and since nothing too exciting is happening, I guess I haven't much to say.*

*Thanks again for the goodies and I'll be sure to put them to good use.*

*You mentioned a new apartment. Where is it? I hope you have better luck than last time. McLeod has an apartment near the "U" now. Eller is still unemployed and penniless at last report. Well. War is Hell.*

*Your Son,*
*Sgt. Rock*

# 28

# COMBAT IN VIETNAM

I THINK I HAVE MADE it clear that my group in Charlie Company did not suffer long sustained battles similar to what I described on June 19th. We were harassed by hit and run ambush attacks. We were more the targets of classic guerilla warfare than the Charlie Company originals.

Still, we were out there. We took our casualties. We endured the unrelenting stress of never knowing what was going to happen in the next moment. Our lives were often mind-numbingly dull until the world shattered in an instant.

Along the way we learned some of the damnedest things you could ever imagine. I could tell from a single burst of gunfire from 500 yards out what type of rifle it was. The Chinese AK-47 had a deep chunka-da-chunka sound. The American M-16 made a sharper rat-ta-tat sound. When a bullet from a Viet Cong carbine flew over your head it whined. The AK-47 was more of a hum. And no matter what the weapon was if

My friend Maynard was never able to avoid the nickname "Krebs." For readers under say, sixty, Maynard Krebs was the beatnik character on the Dobie Gillis TV program played effortlessly by Bob Denver who later became the title character on *Gilligan's Island*.

it sounded like a whip cracking it was way too close and you better get down even lower than you were. That whip cracking sound is very disconcerting.

Some of you may wonder how guys are talked into doing this. Why don't more people get right up to that point and say heck with this? I'm not going. And I don't just mean Vietnam. I mean all wars. Why don't more people just run away? Oddly enough, the answer may lie with an odd combination of human nature and the training we all endured at Ft. Lewis.

More than anything, soldiers are trained to do things together. They rely on one another and they are unlikely to break ranks with the group. There is camaraderie in being part of a group, a team, a unit. If everyone is in this together, soldiers will jump out of planes, storm beaches and ride a helicopter into danger. You hang with the group and hang with the group and all of a sudden you are right in the middle of a shooting war. It's an odd combination of tenacity and herd mentality.

Is that courageous? I think to some degree yes. But the real courage is often revealed once the shooting starts. And in my view the motivation often leads back to the group. Many of the casualties taken in Vietnam were soldiers who were trying to help wounded comrades. To me the best of the best are the guys who take risks for a friend. And it goes beyond that in so many ways because courageous actions and sacrifice in battle are almost always driven by personal bonds and higher purposes.

It was stamina more than courage I recall needing one miserable day when we helped carry a wounded soldier to a Medevac helicopter. In a year full of physical challenges for me, this challenge stood out. The battle details are lost in my memory but we had been ambushed, one of our guys was badly wounded and we were in a situation where it was too dangerous for the chopper to land near where he was hit. We wrapped the soldier into a poncho and four of us determined we would carry him out to a relatively safer place so the chopper could land. We knew it wouldn't be easy but I don't think we knew how tough it would be.

It was raining hard. Much of the time we were in thigh deep mud and water surrounded by jungle like foliage. There was no path to where we were headed. We agonized with every step. He was heavy. Our grip on the wet poncho was tenuous at best. Yet somehow I recall with great clarity the sense of absolute righteousness we must have all felt. This was our guy. He was on our team. We could not fail. We had to hang on. We had to move fast. We pushed to and then past our endurance limits.

None of us would quit on this wounded soldier whose name I can't even recall now. Our arms and hands were shaking. Our legs were rubber. But we were doing something so much more important than everything else surrounding us. This guy would never know who carried him to that chopper but he got there with all of us just assuming he would have done the same for us.

The point is guys are more than willing to ignore danger to give aid to a friend, to attack an enemy to help save the group and to fight a battle for the larger principle of helping your country.

This larger principle about country is what was eventually missing in Vietnam. There were so many examples of selfless sacrifice in the very moment of battle. But did our soldiers really have a larger principle to fight for? Not that I noticed. I think of soldiers as pretty noble guys. And then we train them to protectively react to threats aimed at their fellow soldiers and the larger team. But honestly, by 1967 and 1968 no one could really tell us how our actions were helping our country.

The country itself was telling us we weren't helping. In fact, it was turning on us and saying we were part of the problem. It removed that larger principle that motivates soldiers. We were not fulfilling any obligation to America. We were orphans out there on the battlefield without the comfort of knowing we fought for a righteous cause or an appreciative country.

In a word, that sucked. It certainly led to what I have described on these pages as just looking out for ourselves and trying to keep our team safe. In a larger sense it led to anger and disillusionment. I keep harping on our relative youth. We were not starry-eyed kids but we started out pretty idealistic. We wanted in the worst way to think the brave actions we witnessed had some purpose beyond the moment. We wanted desperately to be part of some larger movement to give some meaning to what we were doing. Sadly, it just wasn't there.

Combat comes with its own set of terrors and haunting memories. Combat combined with disillusionment is much worse. I was able to push past this and blend in when I got home. Many Vietnam soldiers came back negatively stereotyped and some did not do well at all.

Alcohol, drugs, violence, divorce, crime, suicide, homelessness. Take your pick. It didn't happen to everyone but it happened quite often. Young soldiers did the right thing in the heat of combat only to be told their sacrifices were meaningless. This was not a recipe for success.

*March 12, 1967*

*Dear Mom,*

*I got your letter today saying it had been an unbelievable three weeks since you've heard from me. I definitely will try to do better.*

*I am enclosing some pictures of me and even a couple of my associates.*

*Nothing going on today so we are just floating around outside Dong Tam. I guess tomorrow we are going back to a place called "Snoopy's Nose" which brings back some not too good memories.*

[Three or four times we went back to Snoopy's Nose. I think even the Brigade operation planners were enthralled with the name just like we were. But enough already. We never accomplished a thing there other than proving ourselves to be lively targets.]

*I wish I could say it's good to be back but of course it isn't and I like this place less and less as time goes on.*

*I haven't as yet read all the stuff you sent with your letters but I'll try to tonight. I have a new Ayn Rand book that has been keeping me off the streets lately.*

*Today I got five letters from Australia and two from the States. At least I'm appreciated somewhere. I'm afraid the young ladies of Sydney took me a little more seriously than I had anticipated but it's no big thing. At least I know the famous "line" has not become rusty here in VN. It's just as deadly as ever. They just couldn't help themselves.*

[Note: My daughters pounced on this letter and demanded to know what that "line" was. There was no line. These are the ravings of a demented smart mouth who was making false claims about his ability to smooth talk girls. Honestly, it was never really a strong point.]

*More later,*
*Son #1*

# 29

# DEALS WITH SELF

WE HAD LOTS OF TIME to think in Vietnam. I confess I probably wasted a lot of that time day dreaming about the future, girls I would know, fast cars I would drive and vague rock star achievements far outstripping my real ambitions at the time. Lots of guys made little religious deals. You get me home Jesus and I promise I will lead a sin free life forever. I wasn't religious and many of my day dreams were laden with sin so that didn't work for me.

But I did make some deals with myself and I can honestly say to a large degree I have lived up to them. None of them are shockers. None of them were all that hard to live up to in the end. They were deals born out of hard times and maybe too much time to think about these things.

First among these deals was a self-commitment that I was not going to be a person who compromised. Let's look at the

I often wore this flak jacket less for protection and more for bug fighting. It came off much faster than a shirt when the red ants came for a visit.

157

circumstances. I got myself into this Vietnam mess. There were a million ways I could have avoided it. I figured out very quickly this was all a horrible mistake and that we were in Charlie's backyard and that we had no business telling him what sort of government he should support. The honorable thing to do might have been to stand up and say I'm done with this. Send me to prison. In fact, two young Charlie Company kids did just that. I didn't have the guts. So here was the deal. I am going to make this one big compromise and hope to survive this Vietnam tour but after that, never again.

So how does that play out later in life? As a journalist I was a real stickler for professional ethics. My motto was always when in doubt, take the high road. I never took freebies and I tried to keep my staff from taking them. I quit my first job in television news because my boss thought it was okay to run for political office and write news stories about his own campaign. It didn't take any major IQ points to know that was wrong.

It also meant I was never a suck-up. It cost me. But I never happily agreed if I didn't agree. In that sense I drove many of my bosses nuts. I was fired by a major broadcast group because I just couldn't play up to the egotistical, micro-managing group head who demanded blind obedience. Sure, along the way there had to be some small compromises but never the big ones. When I retired last year, I am happy to say, I retired with a clean conscience. I don't know if it was because of that little deal or not, but I left feeling good about a forty-five year career where I never rolled over to pressure.

Another little deal I made with myself involved intimidation. Most of you know people in the workplace who try to get their way through bombast and fear. It never worked with me and this probably does date back to Vietnam. As I have said, if they had guns they could certainly make my knees shake. If not, I was generally unmoved. I don't describe myself as a real confident person in general but in my work life I was very confident about my abilities and my ideas. It took a lot more than shouting and stink-eyes to move me.

This may be slightly related to the fact I also have generally been pretty calm and cool in a crisis. This goes beyond crisis decision making I have described elsewhere. To some degree it is me channeling my first company commander Herbert Lind. And there are plenty of military truisms that support staying calm. People who stay calm make the best decisions. In a confrontation, the person who makes the first confident move usually prevails. A lot of double talk to be sure, but still ample evidence that staying cool and collected is going to help you lead the race so to speak.

The last part of all this is a personal mandate to be honest in my dealings with people both in and out of the workplace. And if I'm really honest this could actually predate Vietnam since my mother is that little voice in my head that keeps me on track with this. She nagged about a lot of things when I was very young. She was a grammar demon and a please and thank you nut. But she also schooled us on telling the truth. I guess as a semi-adult in Vietnam I had the time to think through what type of person I would become and this became one of the foundations (I think my dad influenced me on being even-tempered which I am, at least most of the time).

In a way, isn't it odd that a horrible experience like this could help shape so many of the attributes you carried into your adult life? I suspect I would have been fine without this experience in Vietnam but I have to say in all that upheaval a pretty decent set of life principles emerged and served me well. Maybe it was just because I had time to think about my future that I would have probably filled up with other activities as a civilian.

And it's a good thing I didn't make one of those religious deals. I would have been a serious disappointment.

# 30

# THE GROSSEST THING I SAW IN VIETNAM

EACH C-RATION BOX CONTAINED MORE than just food. You got a spoon and a can opener, you got a little four-pack of cigarettes and among these helpful items you got a little single serving size portion of toilet paper. Let's face it. There were no bathrooms when we were out on operations for three and four days at a time. If this is starting to make you just a trifle uncomfortable you have my strong recommendation to skip the rest of this chapter.

So, back to no bathrooms. If nature called, you took your single portion of toilet paper behind a bush and did your business. Since you couldn't really stray far from your fellow soldiers, privacy was something you remembered from your youth and looked forward to when you got home. Privacy didn't exist in the bush. This was way up high on the list of the thousand or so things I really hated about the Army.

The Delta was crisscrossed with rivers, streams, canals and such so we spent a lot of time trying to master the art of crossing the little foot bridges that got the locals from one place to another. It was just a step up from wading. Sometimes the bridges were as simple as a thick single length of bamboo spanning a dozen or so feet across a canal. Sometimes a few bamboo lengths were tied together for extra length and support. The locals scampered across these bridges with practiced ease. They could probably cross these little bridges blindfolded.

Fully loaded infantrymen were quite a different story. We staggered like drunken monkeys across these spans. We were top heavy. We had muddy shoes. We were ungainly. Lots of times we simply fell off. Other times our weight would simply break the bamboo and we would go ass over tea kettle into the leech-filled swamp water below. There were plenty of high comedy moments associated with these foot bridges and I certainly took more than my share of the tumbles.

All this is just a little set up for what we found in one village. We found an actual bridge. It was made from real lumber. It was about ten feet wide and crossed a real stream maybe fifty feet across. It could never support a car but among the Delta foot bridges this was a Cadillac. It even had a strong wooden railing, unheard of on Delta foot bridges. And along that strong wooden railing was where this story really gets started.

It wasn't long before my fellow soldiers were eyeing that railing. They were mentally calculating its strength. They noticed it was just about the perfect height. We have already established they had no expectation of privacy and before you knew it several of them had dropped their pants, settled comfortably on that railing and began taking leisurely bowel movements into the water below.

There were plenty of local Vietnamese people watching all this in some dismay but what were they going to do? It would have been a bad idea to start scolding heavily armed American soldiers.

Once this got started, more soldiers followed. As many as four or five troopers at a time found comfort on that smooth round railing. That was when we started to notice a disturbance in the water below. I guess the giant carp in these streams were not all that choosy about what they had for lunch because very soon the water was churning with carp fighting each other for the tumbling human waste arriving from above. It was crudely fascinating to watch these fish roiling around snapping at turds like they were a steak dinner. But then what to me was the unthinkable happened.

The locals had never seen this many huge carp in one place in their lives. This was a call to action. First one, then several more soon after, showed up on the other side of the bridge with fishing poles. They were going to catch these shit-eating carp and take them home to dinner.

Okay, now we were grossed out. A few minutes before this bridge had been a picturesque little rural agrarian scene with sampans and little old ladies in coolie hats. Now it was an e. coli nightmare unfolding before our very eyes.

It was like one of those high school charts depicting the water cycle, but it wasn't water that was getting cycled through the environment. I only wish there were TV vampires from True Blood who could glamour away this entire memory.

*March 15, 1968*

*Dear Mom —*

*I got another letter from you today, again saying that you haven't heard from your "little boy" but I have been writing and I will continue to do so. I don't know if the mail is messed up or what but you're bound to get some of these.*

*I'm up listening to my old happy radios tonight and rather at peace with the world since I'm not in the field today. I went down below for a while ago to dig through the canned goods you sent me for some cashews and I found the Almond Roca that I had inadvertently forgotten. So it was a pleasant surprise and I am munching away happily.*

*The old news articles were well written even if they weren't exactly current.. I'm still all wrapped up in* Atlas Shrugged *right now.*

*Before I left I bet Bob Fawcett* [Father of my longtime friend Dave Fawcett] *by the way that Nixon would be the Republican nominee this year. You might remind him.*

*As far as this war goes, the more I think about it the less I can see anything of value in its future. True I suppose we must oppose communism somehow but the more I look into the real facts leading to our presence here I begin to wonder sometimes if we have any business here or not. If it were a case of the North invading the South it would be a simple issue and we would be here with all our virtue but it's not at all a case like that.*

[The pendulum keeps on swinging.]

*A somewhat illogical analogy of what the situation in South Vietnam is would be if the Democrats were in office and the Republicans tried to take over the White House with guns instead of "peaceful elections?" like we try to use. Can you spot a Republican or a Democrat on the street? Nor can you a Viet Cong.*

*The South Vietnamese government, army and whole political structure make Cosa Nostra look like a bunch of pre-schoolers.*

*The Army of South Vietnam is just a payroll burden since they like nothing better than to sit back and watch the Yankee Dogs fight the war and on an individual basis the South Vietnamese soldier generally fights on the side that is winning.*

*The real shocker is that roughly 75% of the people in South Vietnam sympathize with the National Liberation Front movement.*

*Despite all this we still are committed to assist the South Vietnamese government I don't object to it in that sense at all.*

[Note: Again, how could I be saying we needed to help the South Vietnamese government? It was obviously corrupt. It would obviously fold without our support. And it had no vision for the future of the people of Vietnam other than keep that money flowing and keep them in office. I think at this point I must have been fully turned against our war in Vietnam but I couldn't quite admit it in letters home. I certainly wasn't trying to fool my mom since she was definitely not what anyone would call pro-war. Was I trying to keep fooling myself? I can't answer this but it does make me curious reading back to what might have been in my head fifty years ago.]

*What I object to is the methods we use to employ our commitment. Using typical American stubbornness we say that since the National Liberation Front exists and is our enemy we will not recognize its existence. It's sheer stupidity on our part to refuse to recognize the existence of the organization we are fighting against.*

*The only way peace will ever be achieved here will be through recognizing and dealing with the NLF. The North Vietnamese do not feel they have invaded South Vietnam, they feel they are helping liberate it through the NLF to once again unify Vietnam as one country. The 1954 Geneva Agreement calls for two major divisions of Vietnam not two separate countries. The objective of North Vietnam is to unify one race and one culture that has been unified for close to a thousand years.*

*They say that this war is North versus South but how can it be when better than half the people in the South are with the enemy. This is what makes the situation so impossible.*

[I'm rambling here but none of this got past my Mom. She was totally engaged in news and public discourse throughout her life and if I had saved her responses to my various political views that would be obvious. She read papers and magazines including the New Yorker every week for more than sixty years. Later in life she became a huge fan of CNN and PBS. She called me almost every week to tell me how smart her cousin Charley McDowell was on PBS's Washington Week in Review. She begged me to watch although I seldom had time. So, even though I worked in the media throughout my life I was never as well informed as she was.]

*Certainly we can continue to win on the battlefield because believe it or not, American soldiers are a pretty tough lot and can handle themselves well but what do we achieve? We can't kill everybody. The South Vietnamese economy would collapse if the war ended as would their political structure. There is plainly no military end to this war and there will be no end through political means until somebody has sense enough.*

*We aren't wrong for being here but the idea of winning is hopeless and the status quo will remain the same, we will continue to fight, although we can't lose because we are at least powerful enough to take care of ourselves.*

*Well, I'm sure none of this makes any sense because the days of competent letter writing I fear are over. So far I've filled page after page with random thoughts with no real solution.*

*Personally I will continue my useless crusade over here and return a civilian and try to regain an objective view of the whole thing.*

*Do you ever wonder just how much old Lyndon and his boys tell us and how much they don't? I don't feel misguided or brainwashed but I know one thing for certain. I'm tired of being the pawn in somebody else's game and when I get out of what I got myself into, without any large regrets, I am going to do things my way and lead my own game for a while. I'll be the one that decides my fate and this undefined mass of humanity they call upon me to defend or aid can be damned or look after themselves individually. I'm afraid I wasn't cut out to be one of the world's selfless givers.*

*It does look at times ridiculous to see a fairly intelligent man come ten thousand miles to risk his neck for some un-asking and unappreciative and completely unknown person who knows only one word — Gimme.*

*I've been on the wrong end of the gimme's for a while now and it's done one thing for me. I am less likely to ask anyone for anything at all and it may sound tragic to you but I'm a lot less likely to give.*

*I must sound like a complete malcontent but I'm not really objecting to my situation. I'm merely learning from it.*

*Regardless of what it sounds like I still feel justified in being here and perhaps foolishly enough, I'm still not sorry I'm here.*

*I better end this while I have the chance. I'll probably write tomorrow and refute everything I've said tonight but that's war I guess.*

*Love and such,*

*Your Son #1*
*Bill*

# 31

# 2014 REUNION IN D.C.

IN 2014 I WAS RUNNING WJLA-TV in Washington D.C. It's a large broadcast and cable complex where I was responsible for more than three hundred employees. I was a busy guy bombarded with several hundred emails almost every day. I could blow out 20 or 30 emails at a time with just cursory glances when I got backed up. That's why it was almost a miracle that I noticed the email from the National Geographic inviting me to a film screening.

It was the type of courtesy invitation I generally ignored. This one just caught my eye with a picture of soldiers in Vietnam. The title "Brothers in War" seemed generic enough but the picture looked like what we did in the Delta so I read on. It said it was the story of Charlie Company. No big deal. There could have been thousands of Charlie companies in Vietnam. I was not prepared for what I learned next.

In fact, gobsmacked is a good word for how I felt when I read the critical line. Right there in simple type it said this was the story of Charlie Company, 4th of the 47th Infantry, 9th Infantry Division. It was my old company out of all those thousands.

Promotional shot for "Brothers in War" shown on the National Geographic Channel.

"Holy shit!"

Someone had made an hour and a half documentary about my old infantry company. They had pieced together archival films, soldier photos and home movies. Most importantly, it was a narrative of haunting contemporary interviews with a dozen or so former soldiers from the unit. The film was narrated by Charlie Sheen of *Platoon* fame in this context. It told the whole story of these young draftees training together, going to war together and then suffering enormous casualties.

Remember, I was a replacement who joined this group eight months into its tour. I missed many of the major battles that claimed so many of these lives but I knew the survivors and felt to some degree part of it all.

Here's part of what military.com wrote about the film:

> *The tour was brutal and Charlie Company suffered a casualty rate of over 80%, with 26 killed and 105 wounded. The film captures the camaraderie the men developed before going into explicit detail about their major engagements with the Viet Cong. Brothers in War follows the men through their return home in January 1968.*

As I read on I learned more. The film was based loosely on a book called *Boys of '67: Charlie Company's War in Vietnam*. Historian Andrew Wiest had learned of this story when a soldier spoke to his college class about Vietnam. His subsequent book captured all the significant events experienced by the Charlie Company soldiers that later translated into the documentary. I had known nothing about the book.

My voyage of email discovery continued as I read on to learn that the event on the invitation was a private screening of the film at the National Geographic headquarters here in D.C. But the real news was even more exciting. There would be a reception prior to the screening where Charlie Company vets from all over the country would be in attendance. This was amazing and even a little scary. Most of my friends were replacement soldiers like I was and I sort of doubted many of the original Charlie Company group would even remember me. But there was no way I was going to miss this event.

Try to imagine what it was like to be sitting at work one day and learning that a long suppressed and half-forgotten era of your life was about to come back to life. It was like someone lifting the lid off a box you had left on the shelf seemingly forever. Honestly, my initial reaction was total amazement that anyone had kept the story alive all these years. Then the idea of seeing my former fellow soldiers was surprisingly very appealing. I realized this group had been in touch with each other throughout the ensuing decades while replacements like me had dropped out of sight. But certainly I would know someone. And then there was the nervous part. What would it be like to see all these people and see all these images on a big screen?

I took my wife and son to the reception because I think we were all curious. My wife was always interested in my history and my son has been a lifelong amateur military historian including three summer internships at the War College here in D.C. while he was a student.

The event was very much as billed. There were familiar faces I could not put together with names. We had a brief conversation with another former radio guy who had introduced himself. There was a lot of pleasant head-nodding and smiling. And then I ran smack into former Captain Herbert Lind.

Lind was our company commander when I first arrived in Vietnam. He had been awarded a Silver Star for his courageous actions in the battle of June 19, 1967. I think all the soldiers looked up to him for that and many other reasons. He was very cool under fire but he was also very fair-minded and soft-spoken. He was smart, humble and he had a sneaky sense of humor. When I first met him I thought instantly that this was the best kind of guy West Point could produce. Much later I learned he had gone to a small, Midwestern college and attended OCS after he enlisted in the Army. He just seemed to find his calling as an Army officer.

Charlie Company's Commanding Officer Herb Lind in 1967 and 2014.

We had a great conversation. Our six or seven year age difference which was so dramatic in Vietnam had vanished over the decades. We were two old guys who reconnected instantly. He was a much larger figure in my life than I had been in his but we talked about people and events and our current lives in a manner unaffected by all the missing years. Our wives talked and showed the old pictures of us in front of the "Death to the V.C." sign we had all posed in front of back in the day. He was intrigued by my son who spoke Mandarin and had been to grad school in China. I was intrigued by how well he remembered the officers who had replaced him as company commander and for whom I had packed that radio all that time.

I even teased him about one scary night we had experienced way back. Cloud cover had blotted out the stars. It was absolutely dark. We had set up a loose perimeter and thought we were down for the night when we got word we had to move. There was another of those intelligence reports that the area was teeming with Viet Cong and we needed to move to a more defensible position since an attack seemed imminent.

Moving through Viet Cong infested territory at night seemed like a horrible idea. Honestly, it was a horrible idea. Remember, Charlie owned the night. This was his home turf. We were loud, large and easy targets. We were also hugging the ground somewhat fearfully at that point when Captain Lind wandered up to us telling jokes.

"You guys gotta be on your toes like a midget at a urinal," was one I recall.

"Charlie out there is slicker than deer guts on a doorknob," was another.

We were trying to tell the Captain to get down on the ground. He was a huge target. We were scared and he was acting like he was at a backyard barbecue.

"Mullins," he said to one of the soldiers. "Your squad leader says you are clumsier than a cub bear trying to play with himself."

Sometimes when you are in no mood for humor things can be far funnier than they might be in other situations. The Captain walked off into the night and left us all laughing our asses off and wondering if the Viet Cong could hear us. By then we were almost taunting Charlie to hear us laughing. We moved. We survived and life went on.

Captain Lind admitted that night in D.C. he had learned dozens of these little similes fighting forest fires as a summer job in college. We had a good laugh. I told him that meeting up with him again had been the highlight of my evening. He said getting back together with me had been the highlight of his evening as well. I can honestly say that was a very moving moment for me. It's hard to put this in any kind of real perspective anyone else might understand. We hadn't seen each other in 45 years. He had always loomed as a larger than life person who had just proven himself a regular guy.

Herbert Lind died a year or so later following a long battle with cancer. He was an unlikely role model for me but his influence on the person I became in life was considerable. I don't want to get all lofty here but he was a great citizen. He quietly did difficult jobs without complaint. He had a helping hand for the people around him. He left a wake of admirers behind him, particularly those of us who served under him in Vietnam.

This is what I wrote to his wife Becky after he died:

*Dear Becky and Family,*

*I was very sad to learn about Herb's death this week. I don't know if you remember me but I was a replacement soldier who met you and re-connected with Herb at the Geographic screening last year. I have spent most of my life running television newsrooms which I still do at WUSA-TV here in Washington D.C.* [I had changed jobs since the screening.]

When we talked at that event we discussed Herb's un-questionable bravery but I think now I may have missed the bigger picture. Herb was more than brave. He was a great leader. He would always look after his guys. He would never ask anyone to do something he wouldn't do himself. He was a straight-shooter. He would give you an honest answer. You never worried about a hidden agenda. And always, always, he was cool under pressure.

I was describing Herb to my 25 year-old son the other night and a little light bulb went off. These were the very things I tried to do in my various leadership positions. I certainly wasn't perfect but it could very well be a reason I am still working in a youthful and competitive environment while approaching my 68th birthday. I'm not sure I ever consciously followed Herb's example but looking back now I have to believe he must have made a lasting impression on me.

I have quite honestly tried to push Vietnam out of my mind during my adult life. I took my family to the Vietnam Memorial a few times but tried not to dwell on it. My only contact with former soldiers was attending that event where we saw the Charlie Company film. I'm so glad I went. I got to see all those familiar faces. And I was reminded that Herb was a good man, a brave man, a wonderful leader and in the end, an excellent role model.

With respect,

Bill Lord

Charlie Company 1967/68

We went on that night to watch the film about our old unit. It was a gut-wrenching evening for all of us. Even though I arrived in Vietnam after many of the battles depicted in the film, the sights and sounds were all too familiar. The faces of the soldiers telling the stories were familiar. The depictions of friends dying violent deaths and the visits to the Vietnam Wall brought tears to the eyes of even the most stoic of those attending. It was difficult to watch but it was a lasting memorial to those who did not come home and a long overdue tribute to those who did.

Late in the film a former squad leader named John Young eloquently described some of the dilemmas he and other soldiers faced in Vietnam. Remember that night I was sent on the listening post as a scared brand new rifleman? He was the guy who sent me. Here's what he said 45 years later.

> *I was very careful about who I selected to do those dirty little dangerous jobs that never got any thanks and seemed unnecessarily risky.*
>
> *Who was I going to send?*
>
> *Am I going to send...the veterans who have been with me for a year and a half who have fought beside me and bled alongside me?*
>
> *Or am I going to pick on a rookie, a guy whose name I don't even know, a replacement?*
>
> *What's the right thing to do there? What's the right thing? I don't have the answer to that.*
>
> *I do know...I gave the replacements the short end of the stick.*
>
> *And that's just tough. I wasn't going to risk any of my old-timers if I didn't absolutely have to.*

To me this was amazing. Here is a guy after decades still thoughtfully examining the decisions he was forced to make in Vietnam. He wasn't a general making lofty decisions affecting faceless thousands. This was a fellow grunt and draftee facing something much more difficult. His decisions were immediate and personal. If things went wrong he would have to own them vividly forever. These potential life and death decisions were quietly made at the lowest possible levels every day in Vietnam. John Young's interview clearly demonstrates they were not taken lightly.

He sums it up at the end of the film very well.

> *"There's no good option to take. And I'd really rather not have anybody who hasn't been through something like that pass judgment on me.*
>
> *"Don't be too sure about the decision you would have made. And don't be smug about your morality until you've had it tested."*

Here's a message for John Young fifty years later. If I had been in his shoes I would have sent the new guy, too. The older guys had earned the pass. I would get some breaks many months later when I had more mileage under my belt. It is all clear to me now.

The film "Brothers in War" and the book "The Boys of '67: Charlie Company's War in Vietnam" stirred up a lot of buried feelings for me. My picture actually appeared in a group photo near the end of the film. Since then, I have tried to be a little more thoughtful about what happened and how I reacted to Vietnam. I've been a lot more open about it. I've dodged fewer conversations. I'm even writing about it now.

# 32

# MY FIRST VISIT TO THE VIETNAM WALL

I GUESS I COULD START most of these chapters with the term "dopey me" but this one deserves it the most. In the mid-eighties I went to visit the Vietnam Memorial Wall because I was in D.C. and I had been intrigued by the architect, the architecture and by the swirls of criticism over the design. Maya Lin won the contest for designing the Memorial only to have military and political leaders at the time climb down her throat. Where were the statues? Where was the glorification of our fighting men? Why dig below ground to put up this wall of names? To traditional thinkers this Memorial made no sense. The Secretary of the Interior at the time, James Watt, even tried to refuse a building permit for the Memorial.

So I thought I was going to check out this structure to assess the design and the dispute that actually had continued. This would

The Vietnam Wall, 2017.

have been in 1984 or 1985 so the Memorial had only been open a couple of years. This "dopey me" approach to thinking my visit was about the design left me totally unprepared for the gut punch I was about to experience. I thought, stupidly, I was a tourist.

We were in D.C. for a happy event. A story I had reported won a Robert F. Kennedy Award for Reporting on the Disadvantaged. I was working on a documentary program in Salt Lake City at the time and when we realized that by winning the award we were invited to a presentation party at Hickory Hill, the Kennedy residence in McLean, Virginia, we weaseled our way into a free trip to D.C. at the expense of our employer.

We arrived at Hickory Hill determined to act like visiting the Kennedys was just another day at the office for hotshots like us. There was a sign by the door that said something like "Beware of Large Dog Inside" and sure enough, there was a giant sleeping Newfoundland by the door. As we walked through the reception line at the entrance several people congratulated us on winning the award. There were dozens of people there and I believe only five winners so we were impressed they had all done their homework to know the names of the winners. Or so we thought. By the time Ethel Kennedy congratulated us I said something to that effect and she just laughed and said no, we didn't do any extra work. The name tags were all color coded.

Hotshots, indeed.

Despite my rube like entry, it was a fascinating night. Ethel Kennedy could not have been a more congenial hostess. Joseph Kennedy III was there hanging around and talking to us like we were serious players. Several of Bobby and Ethel Kennedy's kids were on hand but there were so many of them I can't remember which ones. Senator Ted Kennedy showed up and stood out in the garden with a group of us for what seemed like nearly an hour just talking about the important events of the day although I can't remember now what they were.

Still, this was pretty amazing stuff for any up and coming journalist and I must say they couldn't have been more supportive of our work. We were almost treated like royalty (we were not, as Donald Trump says today, enemies of the American people). The Kennedys present at this event encouraged everyone there to continue to use our profession to be a voice for those who had no other means of seeking justice. It was pretty inspiring. I have done my best to live up to that promise.

At any rate we had plenty of time before our flight home the next day and were off to the Wall like any other tourists. We walked across the National Mall, turned right where the pavement started to decline and walked in.

And then it just hit me. As it was designed, I saw my own reflection in the stone where all the names are chiseled. I later learned this was to connect the present and the past. And I just looked at all those names and sort of crumbled. I am unable even now to fully describe what happened. I just couldn't move. I can't believe I didn't see this coming but I didn't. I had trained myself from way back in Vietnam not to be emotional and without thinking about it I had assumed somehow this little tourist stop would be no big deal.

I looked around at people rubbing names with paper and crayons as remembrances. There were plenty of guys in my general age group walking alone deep in contemplation. Some wore caps with insignias on them. There were and still are retired military types there to talk and help find names of fallen friends. I saw medals and unit patches left on the ground as tributes to lost friends and family members.

Years later my friend Mike Goldfein did a television story at the warehouse where the National Park Service stores and catalogues every offering left at the wall. The most memorable to me was the brand new Harley-Davidson motorcycle with the license plate "HERO" on the back. There was money. There were teddy bears, letters, various military items and countless other individual gestures, grand and small. Fascinating stuff.

I stood in the middle of all this half-blubbering, speechless and a little embarrassed. My colleague who was with me sensed my discomfort and walked ahead. But I wasn't really alone. Surrounding me were people of all stripes feeling the same emotions. The place clearly lends itself to reflection and outpourings of pent up feelings. It is deeply personal as I am sure it was intended to be. It honors the dead as I did when I found Bob Nardelli's name. But it also provides some refuge for the living. It is a place you can go to feel the multitude of emotions that swell together when the Vietnam War is contemplated. I can't say it provides comfort because there really can be no comfort in what this Memorial represents. It was just a place to pay your respects in a very personal way and to me that is its genius.

The World War II Memorial opened some years later as I was living in D.C. It beautifully captures the power of America. Its state by state monuments speak to the ability we have to pull together in a crisis and in this case save the world from tyranny. I love that we have almost daily honor flights where World War II veterans now in their mid-90's are flown in to be honored at this Memorial. But it's a monument to America.

The Vietnam Memorial is different. It's a personal tribute to each and every name on the wall. It is a place where anyone can come and contemplate all the soldiers or individual soldiers. It makes no attempt to glorify Vietnam. It serves only to allow us to remember what happened in Vietnam and the people who were there.

So hats off to Maya Lin and the Park Service folks who selected this design and then stuck with it through the battles that followed. The Memorial has stood all the tests of time and continues to be among the most popular public places in America. By honoring each individual in perpetuity we are slowing striking a balance against the lack of honors Vietnam soldiers were granted when they came home, those who died and those who did not.

# 33

# DORFMAN

## THE GUY WHO MIGHT HAVE
## SAVED MY LIFE.

DORFMAN. SMART KID. I SAY kid because in my memory he's still a whip smart, teenaged company clerk from New York City. He must be seventy by now. In those days he was a living example of what we called Remington Rangers. All Army clerks were named after their typewriters. This was not a compliment but he embraced the title in much the way we embraced being called grunts. If you need to conjure up an image of Dorfman think of a wise-cracking, Jewish, Radar O'Reilly. He swam happily in the oceans of Army paperwork.

I can only hope Dorfman has led a full life with all the joys of family, good health and money falling into his pockets. I am embarrassed that I can't recall his first name. I believe it was Daniel but I can't be sure. Dorfman was one thing I could never be once I left Vietnam. He was a detail guy. He read the fine print. His love of the power of paperwork also had a stunning effect on my life.

"Lord, I think I've found a way to get out of Vietnam three months early," he confided as he wandered by one day.

"Sure," I said. "Sell me some swampland in Florida first." I may have even asked what he had been smoking since fantasies aside we all believed getting out early was about as likely as water buffaloes taking a leisurely flight across the rice paddies.

"I'm serious," he said. "I stumbled on this thing called the Early Release Program. You can go home early if you get accepted to college. It also works if you can get job in a defense industry. I could be back in the world, three months ahead of schedule."

"Dorfman," I said. "Tell me more."

Now I knew Dorfman was excited by this process. He was doing it for himself. Nobody in their right mind wanted to stay any longer than absolutely necessary. But I don't think he realized right away how loudly those bells were exploding in my head. It took me less than a nanosecond to do the math. I was just a few weeks away from that "three month" deadline. I knew I would be accepted at my old community college with just a phone call. It was a public school. It accepted everyone.

I also had one more ace up my sleeve. I once had worked in a defense industry and I still had an active top secret security clearance. Go ahead, laugh. What lowlife grunt in 1968 has a top secret security clearance? Heck, I was laughing. And here's why. One of my earlier college jobs was working as a part-time mail boy at the Boeing Company in Seattle. I'm sure the title has been cleaned up over the years but basically I drove around the airplane factory in a golf cart and dropped off mail throughout the huge complex where 707's were born. Some of the mail was classified so anyone delivering the mail had to have a security clearance.

I came clean right away. I told Dorfman I wanted to try this myself. He shared all the documents and all the forms. Remember, he was the detail guy. He knew all the military channels we would use to route our applications. He was solid gold. We also made a pact. We would work on this together but not tell anyone else until our applications went through.

Boy, did I write some letters that night.

*March 19, 1968*

*Dear Mom,*

*I just have time for a quick note.*

*I need ——*

*1.) A letter of acceptance from the Dean of Admissions of any college in the U.S.A. (Highline or Shoreline JC will do) for summer quarter and on this letter it should state the last day I could possibly register for summer (yes, summer) quarter.*

*2.) My reason for trying to get back in school for summer quarter is to get my required subjects over with so I can pick up the normal sequence of studies for my degree in the fall. I need letters from "Captains of Industry" suggesting that if I complete my courses (my major will arbitrarily be Political Science) I could or would be employed by the Boeing Company at some menial task with an important title or nomenclature.*

*This may sound like a joke but I'm dead serious. We may have to stretch the truth a bit but we must convince the Pentagon that I should attend summer quarter this year to round out my educational bag.*

*The reason for all this is simple. It would eliminate the necessity of me remaining in Vietnam getting shot at for the summer when I should be improving my already demented mind. Since logical thinking doesn't allow me to be in two places at one time then I'll have to get a three month early-out from the Armed Service for reasons of attending school.*

*I'm quite serious about this and I can't emphasize its importance that you do these things since the three months difference would mean three months of not dodging bullets.*

*The thing I did wrong is allow these people to think I do a good job in the field so they are going to keep me "on the line" so to speak for my entire tour.*

*My opinion of this: @!E&$3#*

*Immediate action on your part is requested.*

*Humbly,*

*Your son — the chicken*

My mom was not perfect and sometimes not even reliable. Give credit where credit is due, she took the ball on this one and ran. I think I had been so self-absorbed over my own issues in Vietnam I probably had failed to think through what it was like for my mother. I was named after my mother's brother, William Hoffman. As the one boy in a family with three sisters he was adored by them throughout his life. Like so many bright young men of his age he enlisted in 1942 and then threw himself into one of the most dangerous occupations in World War II. He was a B-24 navigator flying bombing missions over Europe. He knew the odds and answered the call. He was killed in a bombing raid over Frankfurt, Germany in February, 1944. His picture was always present in our house growing up yet I didn't really connect the dots on her grief from losing him and the worries she must have had twenty some years later with a son on the front lines of this crummy little war in Asia.

She never burdened me with her feelings about all this and even now I feel like I could have and should have been much more compassionate.

This could very well have been one of the reasons she saved all my letters and didn't tell anyone about them. There may have been that voice in the back of her head that told her that these letters, like the ones from her brother a generation ago, could be all that she would have left if something terrible happened.

At any rate, she got busy to get her son home and I was appreciative. Did I feel like I was running away? No. Maybe I wasn't as brave as my namesake but I felt I had put in my time and now it was someone else's chance to step up.

*March 22, 1968*
*Dear Mom,*

*As you can tell from my last letter I'm absolutely insane but I intend to make every try in the world to do this early discharge deal.*

*The plan is to go summer quarter at one of the JC's and transfer to the "U" in the fall. All I really need to get out is the letter of acceptance to the school around June 5 and a few letters recommending approval for my early discharge from various important sounding people stating the necessity of getting me educated.*

*It may not work but it's certainly worth a good try and I'd really appreciate it if you'd look into it immediately because I have to get the papers of acceptance and recommendation back soon to give the Army plenty of time to choke them down and approve them. Please don't put it off till tomorrow. This is an emergency.*

*The last few days we spent in a graveyard, supposedly defending an artillery base but all we ended up doing is laying in the sun. We build a cool bunker in some old shrine that looked to have been there for hundreds of years.*

*We're going out again in the morning since these people don't seem to believe in resting the horses anymore but somehow we survive.*

*The more time I spend in this place the more of a dissenter I become. If you could only see how pointless and how hopeless this situation is over here.*

[I guess I finally hit that tipping point where I was no longer making excuses for our presence here. As you have been noting throughout all of my experiences, all of the contemporary events and all of the feedback from others had finally convinced me we were making a colossal mistake. I don't know if I came to that conclusion independent of this new opportunity for an early out. I suspect not. I think like so many others, I had just plain had enough of this war on every level.]

*If you give a dog a bone he'll want every bone you've got and if you don't give him the rest he'll bite the hell out of you until you give. That's the way it is here and they can't realize that respect is never won by giving people what they are too lazy to get themselves and making sniveling beggars out of them because it beats working.*

*Anyway please get on top of some school (HJC is fine) and get me that letter of acceptance and registration date for summer quarter. Also don't tell everybody about it because it's still in the dream and doubtful stage. It's worth a try though because other guys have done it so quicker we get done the better the chance.*

*I'll let you know the progress as things go along.*

*It needs approval from company, battalion, brigade and the division before it goes through. So far I maybe have company approval if I hurry before we change COs.*

*More later,*
*Bill*

COMMUNITY COLLEGE DISTRICT IX

## HIGHLINE COLLEGE

MIDWAY, WASHINGTON 98031

March 28, 1968

To Whom It May Concern:

Mr. William H. Lord has expressed his desire to
return to Highline College during the summer quarter
1968/1969.

Since he was a matriculated student at Highline
before, all he must do for summer quarter to be accepted
is register for his classes *before* June 28, 1969.
Summer quarter registration will begin on June 5, 1968
and end on June 28, 1968. Classes will start on June
24, 1968.

Sincerely yours,

*Karen Thompson*

(Miss) Karen Thompson
Registration Secretary

KLT:kt

Mail took forever in those days but in less than two weeks this
letter arrived welcoming me back to college.

The next letter to arrive was what I still call a masterpiece. Here's
a little background. I got the mail boy job because my mom raised us
as a single mother on the salary she made as a secretary to one of the
Boeing Vice-Presidents. From her perch on executive row she knew
just about everyone of consequence in the company. For much of my
life I have downplayed using connections or "networking" and all that
insider stuff. On this occasion I was shameless. My mom tracked
down someone in Personnel whose title might have been Military
Service Administrator to write a letter on my behalf. To be honest,
they may have just made up that title but it sure looked good on that
Boeing stationary. I never felt so official in my life. I was upgraded to

a Communications Specialist. The letter sort of implies I was re-employable in a defense plant without mentioning I had been a half-stoned, surly, long-haired freak carelessly driving a golf cart through the airplane factory. I call it a masterpiece because it seemed to imply so much while saying almost nothing. I wonder as I write this today if they really did make up that title. I bet they did.

We were off to the races. We filled out all the forms and sent them all off. It was very much like a modern day college application but without those horrible essays. Dorfman tracked it all. We were approved at the company and then battalion level. We squirmed as we waited to hear what was happening at the division headquarters where the ultimate decision would be made.

Then the bombshell hit.

Dorfman put on a good face. He congratulated me. I had been approved. With the passage of time I now had a flight home scheduled in less than one month rather than nearly four months. I was going to survive this miserable war. I was going back to the world. I was going back to school. It was amazing. I have always said there is no drug that compares to the adrenalin rush that comes after you survive a brush with serious danger. This approval produced the seismic version of that adrenalin rush.

But not for Dorfmam. His paperwork did not come back with mine. It wasn't denied. It just wasn't decided yet. His departure date was some weeks farther out from mine so they may not have been under the gun to get his done as quickly. At any rate, my joy was muted by his disappointment. This was his train I had jumped aboard. I was going home and he was sitting on pins and needles waiting for word.

I checked with him just before I flew off to Bien Hoa for my flight home. There was still no word. I then boarded what we called the freedom bird and as was the case with everyone, lost touch forever.

I have told myself over the years that of course Dorfman's paperwork must have come back approved. I can only hope he got home safely and quickly. At the very least, thank you, Dorfman. We can never really know, but you just might have saved my life.

*May 10, 1968*
*Dear Mom,*

    *With unprecedented swiftness and uncanny lack of good sense the Army has mistakenly approved my early discharge.*

*My original day to get out was September 12 and the maximum early out would be June 17. From what I can tell now I should come tripping in around the 22nd or 23rd but I don't know for sure yet.*

[My good fortunes seemed to be on a roll. As it turned out they sent me out sometime around June 9th or 10th. I don't have the exact date but it was earlier than I first thought.]

*I still am in a daze of disbelief since these things are usually sent in and never seen again but in this case it only took nine or ten days and they were right back with their seal of approval.*

*It looks like I'll be able to register myself but if I don't get back in time you can do it for me. I want to take English 102 for sure but anything else I'd be shooting in the dark just taking what's available. I want to take a Business Administration class (the lowest one with credit) and possibly some very low form of mathematics. I might even take a PE class—who knows. At any rate I should be there in time to do it.*

*Next problem — Since it's rather obvious that for my first few weeks of civilian life I will have no license, no insurance and above all no car and no place to live. It's going to take a while to scout out this driving business and purchase the suitable vehicle (sports car of course) so I'm going to be forced to live within walking distance of old HJC.*

*Could you possibly check around that area for something very cheap for me to rent. I want to live alone for the summer and I'll go 80 or 90 a month if we can't find anything cheaper. I'll only need the place till the 1st of September or so because I plan on UW in the fall. By then I should have the other stuff straightened out. I know there is a trailer park just behind the college and there is a motel (Mt. Baker I think is the name) that rents an apartment across the highway. Also across the highway there used to be some one room shacks that rented out. Remember I'm used to living in a jungle and am not too hard to please. If you can find a roof to cover my head for the summer near the school, I'll pay and thank you even.*

*Meanwhile I'm still pinching myself trying to realize I only have about 30 more days in this rotten place. I really want to thank you for all the running around you have done and probably will still be doing but don't think I don't appreciate all of it. I may even quit smoking dope.*

[I reveled in talking about drug use with my mom and I never failed to exaggerate it. It was all part of my filial duty to try to make the parent uncomfortable. She was such a pro at needling me it only seemed fair to needle back.]

*I'd still like you to remain sort of silent about my coming and then I can make it all a little surprise when I make my grand entrance.*

*Well Ma, I end this now — Ignore the newspapers and stick by the phone come June and I'll call from the airport.*

*Son #1,*
*Me*

*P.S. How 'bout a clean and press job on the civilian suit?*

# 34

# DONG TAM TODAY

I ALWAYS WONDERED WHAT HAD happened to our old base camp Dong Tam. The Army Corps of Engineers had created the land by dredging sand from the bottom of the Mekong River on to existing rice paddies. They raised the ground level three or four feet over roughly a mile square area which became home to much of the 9th Infantry Division and at various times our Charlie Company.

It was big enough for barracks, mess halls and even an air strip covered with perforated metal slabs. It was actually a pretty good little military base. Our needs were met.

I'm guessing it was pretty expensive to build but once we left it must have been pretty worthless. It wouldn't grow anything. No one was building shopping malls in Vietnam. There wasn't even a tree growing on the property. So what did the Vietnamese do with it?

Well, thanks to my intrepid son we have the answer. My son is a Foreign Affairs type who has spent a great deal of time in the Far East. During one long vacation through Thailand, Cambodia and Vietnam he went off in search of Dong Tam to satisfy my curiosity. Trust me, none of my guesses or probably yours would be anywhere near the right answer.

He found the local bus from Saigon (now Ho Chi Minh City although everyone still calls it Saigon) south to My Tho and was on his way. The roads are paved now. Even old Highway 1 that stretched the length of the Mekong in Vietnam has some sort of rudimentary pavement. It was pretty much mud, clay and some gravel when we were there.

In My Tho he found that Dong Tam had become something of a local tourist destination. You could go there and see the snakes. That's right. Snakes. It seems a North Vietnamese Army colonel bought the property way back and turned it into a snake farm. It is heralded on the web as a place where venomous snakes are raised so their poisons can be extracted for medical research. Oh, but there is so much more to the story.

The snakes are raised there and the venom is extracted to be sure. But forget about the scientific research. The venom is packaged up with various types of liquor for sale in individual doses or in bottles of snake wine. Is it for science? Nope. The Dong Tam Snake Farm is a purveyor of sexual performance elixirs sold in all of Asia. Could it be that wine and whiskey with a couple of drops of cobra venom can give you a big throbbing woody? That's the popular belief. It seems all the rage throughout China and the South East Asia peninsula. It is an Asian equivalent to Viagra but I'm guessing without the television commercials of hot babes tossing a dose into the suitcase heading out for that getaway weekend.

It was a fifty year transition from basecamp to the bedroom, all compliments of the U.S. Army Corps of Engineers. And thanks to my son for clearing that up for us.

*May 29, 1968*

[Note: By May 29, 1968 I was what was called "short" in Vietnam. I was about to return to the world. Everybody caught a break when they were short. There was a collective effort to ensure no one faced any unnecessary danger in the last few weeks they were in country.]

*Dear Mother,*

*Yes it's me again, your pot head son signing on with another cheerful message from the land of the Sky Blue Waters. What are you up to anyway? I just heard the result of the Oregon fiasco and I hope you are prepared to join the new radical political group I am forming.*

[I have no idea what happened in Oregon.]

*This typewriter has had the course I'm afraid.*

*The truth of the matter is Vietnam is not such a bad deal when you don't have to go out to the field and be a grunt. Now I work about three hours a day on a bad day and I have no real responsibility except to pass out batteries to the radio men every three days and for this I still get the same pay as when I was working. I'm signing all my letters Sgt. W.H. Lord Ret. and pretty soon I'll just drop the Sgt. part and be plain old retired. Yes Mom it's hard to believe that in two short weeks I'll be back on campus smoking dope with the rest of the guys.*

*Have you found any place for me to stay yet? I require at least a lean-to to keep the rain off my head. Are there any new bars open that I should know about? It's going to be hard to believe that I am still a child in the eyes of the law but I guess I won't worry about it too much. At least I'll be old enough to vote in November if that means anything.*

*Anyhow Lucy, I shall be home soon and for the rest of the time I'm fairly safe and sound. I'll see you later.*

[I'm thinking now a simple thank you might have been appropriate here although I guess I shouldn't have expected that much from my younger self. At any rate, I did appreciate what she had done and the stories lived on in family lore forever. And the fact that she saved all these letters is a little bit astounding to me. She was not the sentimental type and I honestly did not know they existed until just recently. This was my last letter home from Vietnam and I can see at the very end of the letter I reverted back to calling my Mom by her first name. What the heck does that mean? The pressure is off and I can go back to our old methods of conduct? I couldn't tell you. I'm sure there must be some psychology major out there somewhere to explain that to me.]

*Your Son*

# 35

# COMING HOME

THE TAKEOFF ANGLE WAS DRAMATICALLY steep for a 707 as we took off from Saigon that last time on our way back to the world. I suspect it was one last safety measure against ground fire. As I watched the reflected sun ripple across rice paddies I was struck once again at how beautiful and peaceful it all looked even though I knew for a fact my friends were still down there with their butts on the line.

Once we were fairly certain we were beyond any danger there was a noisy chorus of rebel yells, cheers and high volume shouts of phrases the likes of "Adios, MF's." The pandemonium was unruly and sustained despite polite requests from the Captain to stay seated with our seat belts securely fastened. Like a little turbulence was going to wreck this party. I don't think so.

Our flight plan would take us to Tokyo, Anchorage and ultimately to Travis Air Force Base outside San Francisco where most of us would be released from active service. The call for cocktails began almost immediately.

Yet for all our happiness there was a certain foreboding about the world we would find back at home. Our flight was around June 9th or 10th of 1968. We had learned that Bobby Kennedy had been shot and clung to life for a short time. The way we received news in those days I'm not even sure we knew at that point that he had died. 1968 was already shaping up to be a momentous year. The Tet Offensive we had all endured had fueled the anti-war movement to new heights. Martin Luther King had been murdered. Riots broke out across American cities. President Johnson had announced he would not run for re-election and had started scaling back the war. Bobby Kennedy had become the great hope for many of us. Now he was taken down. There were so many unknowns. We had all hoped to be travelling home to a time warp where *Ozzie and Harriet* and *Leave it to Beaver* were the norms. That was nothing like the world we would re-enter.

The first thing I did upon landing at an air base in California is read all the articles about Bobby Kennedy. It was truly a sobering historical moment in many ways. I was still grateful beyond belief to have survived and to be back on American soil. But to me, Bobby Kennedy represented everything that could still be hopeful about our country and his loss was tragic. In my view, he was the truly exceptional Kennedy who fought tirelessly for a lot of things I thought were important. Who was left to carry that forward? No one came instantly to mind.

Still, I was back. To get a cheap flight I had to wear my uniform on the plane from San Francisco to Seattle. We've all heard the stories of Vietnam soldiers being taunted at airports. That didn't happen to me. It was obvious I was just home from the war but no one got in my face. Despite my paranoia, no one reacted much at all. Needless to say though, I never wore the uniform again. I didn't wear it again but here's a subtle irony. That dusty old uniform is hanging in my closet today fifty years later. I really can't tell you why. It's just hanging there.

I did have some priorities back home. Yes I wanted to see old friends. There must have been girls to see. But I believe the single thing I missed most in my time away was a plain old American hamburger. Not only did I check that box, I had my first Big Mac which I think had arrived on the scene in my absence. So began a lifelong relationship. Someone had created a double decker burger with everything I liked and nothing I didn't like. My last job before retirement was next door to the McDonalds on Wisconsin Avenue in D.C. I was a regular. I think one of the reasons I have never gone to a cardiologist is to avoid having some authority figure telling me to stop. I continue to consume Big Macs to this very day. I guess this also very clearly states that whatever happened to me over this lifetime, I did not ever become what would be considered a serious foodie.

I had $1100 in the bank when I got home. My pay in the Army was about a $100 a month supplemented by a pretty insulting $65 a month in combat pay for serving in Vietnam.

My letters home indicated that I would save this money and use it for college and high-minded purposes like that. And then I saw the car that looked just like the one below. It is still my favorite car ever. It was a well-used, high mileage but smooth running 1960 Austin Healey, black with a red interior just like the one in this picture.

My best guess is that this is a 1961 Austin Healey 3000.

Well, that spend money wisely resolution went out the window in a hurry. But the car was years away from being a collector's item and I found this one for $1000. It had an ever so cool overdrive toggle switch on the dashboard which gave the effect of a high acceleration downshift at freeway speed. There were shiny wire wheels. I was smitten. Screw everything, I want this car. I deserve this car. I don't care if I starve but I have to own this car. In just moments I was down to my last hundred bucks. By the time it was licensed and insured I probably was down to my last couple of twenties.

And there I was, one penniless kid just out of the Army with a chip on his shoulder and ready to face the world. I really did have a "me against the world attitude." And I was cocky. There was never a moment of doubt that I would get through school, find something fun to do with my life and cash in on all the enjoyment I had been denied for the past year. And it was all going to be made ever so much easier now because I had the top down and I was styling in my fancy Austin-Healey. I did love that car. All I had to do now was get my buzz cut to grow out.

Here's another laughable fact. In many ways I felt old. I felt like I had been away from home for a decade and not just under two years. I had been in Europe, Asia, Australia. I had that practiced look of a world weary traveler. I may have even been shaving almost every day by now. But as I have mentioned, I was still a month away from my 21st birthday. I could not go drinking with my friends despite all my trials. They all had sensible, early in the school year birthdays. I wasn't bitter about this but it felt like such a joke to have been old enough to do what I had done but not old enough to buy a beer at a bar. Not to worry, though. We found many less than legal ways to celebrate my arrival home that did not include barstools.

Ultimately, school was my savior. I believe even now that by having virtually no transition between Vietnam and college I didn't have time to dwell on anything. I immediately got too busy for any serious reflection. And school was so much easier this time around. It was amazing to me what you could do if you simply showed up for class. And I was light years more confident in social situations than I had been in my previous attempt at school.

Even though I was older than many of the students, I still looked extremely young and certainly did not stand out in any way other than knowing that I could handle just about anything life threw at me. That came from experiences most of these other college kids would never have. I didn't talk about Vietnam. Few people knew I had even been in the army.

This is where I put my "look forward" attitude to good use. I was either lucky or I made a good choice. I was able to suppress the past, live in the present and work toward future goals. I even allowed my friends to occasionally use a provocative nickname they had for me. Baby Killer. This sounds very odd but in a way this was how my friends covered for me if a conversation drifted into any uncomfortable discussion of Vietnam soldiers.

"Be careful what you say now, Willie's a baby killer, he was in Vietnam," they would say.

It was crude as we all were in those days but it was protective. My high school friends respected what I had been through even if they didn't agree with the war. And they made sure I didn't get sideswiped by people who didn't know my past. It also gave me the perfect opportunity to deny that I was a baby killer, to say that I was just a poor stupid draftee who flunked out of college on the first try. In a way it was a good way for me to be humanized despite the apparent insult.

I breezed through school. I took it seriously because it was a second chance and I made the most of it. Ultimately I transferred to the University of Washington where I drifted into the anti-war movement but with surprising results. I opposed the war for the same reasons that drove my behavior when I was there. We could not win because there was nothing there for us to win. We were being suckered by a corrupt Saigon government to fight its war and keep its leaders in power.

But a college campus in the late sixties was totally polarized. If you opposed the war, you certainly must want to burn down the ROTC building too, right? And if you were for the war, you must be a right wing lunatic who wants to suspend personal freedoms, right? There was no middle ground for reasonable people to inhabit. Or so I thought until one day I just happened to walk into the University of Washington *Daily*, the student newspaper. At the time it was a totally biased pro-demonstrator, anti-war, pardon the expression, rag. But the people there were interesting. Most of them believed in objectivity in reporting. I sort of figured out that here was an opportunity to be right in the middle of the action without being a polarized advocate of something. Somewhere in all this I became a journalist and to a large degree found my calling.

And then Vietnam reached out and touched me again. In the spring of 1970 I was carrying an enormous class load because I was trying to "catch up" with people who had not gone away for two years. President Nixon decided this would be a good time to bomb Cambodia. Campuses around the country erupted including ours. Students marched in the streets, took over administration buildings and generally shut down universities. Four students were gunned down at Kent State University. And at least to some degree, the schools by now were complicit in these shutdowns. The bombings and other war issues were now openly unpopular almost everywhere.

When order was restored two weeks later it was time to get back to class. But what would the university do about grades and missed assignments etc. It was just my good fortune that the University of

Washington declared a total amnesty to students and gave us the option of grading ourselves for that quarter. I was carrying 23 credit hours, half again as many as the usual 15 credit hours needed to stay on track for graduation. What's the correct move here? Do I try to figure out what classes I should give myself a B or do I just give myself A's across the board. I think you see where I'm going here.

I went with all A's. My GPA improved and perhaps even helped me get into grad school at the prestigious Medill School of Journalism at Northwestern University. I might have made it without all those A's but who was going to take that risk?

# 36

# THE AFTERMATH

I HAVE DESCRIBED MYSELF AS lucky in many ways. I didn't have the nightmares, cold sweats or flashbacks some of my colleagues experienced. I am reasonably certain I did not suffer from Post-Traumatic Stress although you never really know. I jumped out of my shoes a zillion times that first Fourth of July I was home much to the amusement of my friends. Loud noises like firecrackers produced an involuntary reaction. But beyond that I was spared many of the traumatizing symptoms that are common even today with veterans returning from the Middle East. That's not to say I was unaffected but my issues were much more manageable than those faced by many of my contemporaries.

My issues were different. I was very protective of my feelings. I really did consciously build a shell. That made much of what I did superficial. I never really engaged in any group activity 100%. If there was a way to stand on the sidelines of any activity, that's where you would find me. Even in my professional life I found a way to be an outsider even in the highly team oriented jobs I had over of the years. And on a personal level, I was a terrible candidate for any long term committed relationships with girls. I liked them just fine. I had several live-in girlfriends along the way. But I kept an emotional distance that must have been frustrating for them but kept me in what I can only call a comfort zone. This is an embarrassing thing to admit but many times I had all the benefits of a real relationship but with none of the long term obligations.

I was also impatient but I can't tell where that came from. All my life I have tried to hurry through whatever I was doing to get on to the next thing. Was this just A.D.D. or somehow related to my unwillingness to even commit to things in the short term. While this was a great crutch for a journalist it may not have been appreciated by kids who wondered why Dad wanted to leave their soccer games at halftime or their musical performances after the first song.

There is another curious aspect of my unwillingness to engage on the subject of Vietnam. Was I just posturing to present myself as a troubled veteran or was it real? I know I made conscious decisions to look forward and not back. It still makes a lot of sense to me. The inability or unwillingness to make commitments and the superficiality of my behavior seems entirely involuntary. But is there a voluntary component to all this working alongside the rest?

I knew quite a few vets who came home and were unable to get on with productive lives. I think in my mind I may have occasionally thought they might have been posturing. Sometimes I wanted to get in their faces a little.

"Get over this. Get on with your life. Look ahead," I wanted to say.

I thought they must have been looking for excuses for any potential failures. That sounds much more insensitive than it is. I wanted them to move forward. I wanted them to succeed. I wanted to help. But I ended up going back to the age old question that if a person acts crazy, are they really crazy?

If these guys were messed up by their experiences and looked for excuses, was that any less real than facing sub-conscious behavior changes? I think my conclusion is that if the experience of serving in Vietnam results in any type of self-defeating behavior, it doesn't really matter if it's driven by conscious or sub-conscious triggers. I am totally unqualified to even discuss this matter but the simple fact is the whole experience changed us in a myriad of ways.

Over the years did I miss the guys in Vietnam? Yes. Did I worry about their well-being? Absolutely. But did I ever contact them? No. It was like a past life, a different and now totally disconnected life. It lacked any relevance in the here and now. We had been thrown together into the alien world of Vietnam and I had somehow survived. I wanted to forget it and was busy suppressing every possible memory or connection to that alien place. That sounds cold and uncaring but in the end that's what somehow worked for me. If pressed, I admit it, I would probably do the same thing all over again. I built a little cocoon around myself that protected me for most of my life.

I always felt that if I survived Vietnam, I wouldn't ask any favors. Survival was the great big favor I could not ever top. No free meals on Veteran's Day, no special stand up and be cheered at sports venues. I didn't even mention Vietnam in job interviews unless I was asked. And I did a pretty good job of this until just recently. As I searched for a parking spot in a crowded lot at my local Harris Teeter grocery store not long ago I pulled into what looked like an open spot. There was a little sign that said This Space for Veterans Only.

Well now, don't mind if I do. Harris Teeter had reserved several parking spaces for veterans. I admit I use them from time to time. I did not feel like I was taking any advantage of anyone. But here's the funny part. Every time I use the spot I expect someone will jump out and ask who I think I am parking there.

One more thought as the boomerang comes around one last

time. Seven or eight years ago my feet started feeling numb. I changed shoes to no avail. I finally ended up with a neurologist who told me I had peripheral neuropathy. It means the nerve signals from foot to brain have slowed down. There's no cure and so far it is an increasing but still minor annoyance.

A couple of years ago we were on a tour in Scotland when a guy about my age told me he had neuropathy. When I told him I had it as well he only asked one question.

"Where did you serve in Vietnam?"

Huh? I told him the Delta and he said, "check it out." He told me there is now a definitive link between peripheral neuropathy and exposure to Agent Orange. The Delta is one of the zones where Agent Orange was used with great regularity. So even after fifty years, Vietnam still has a fang or two in me.

# 37

# THE GIFT

On balance, serving in Vietnam was a horrible experience. It hit lifetime peaks for physical discomfort, fear, resentment and ultimately separation from society. We were traumatized in countless ways. I still walk around today with a mental warehouse filled with bad memories suppressed to the best of my abilities all these years. But, as you may have noticed, there is another side to that coin.

Once I left Vietnam and the military I was a much more confident person. I was determined to set my own steely-eyed agenda for the rest of my days. I was a much better leader. I trusted myself and seldom second guessed my decisions. Overall, I have to admit I was a better person. These things all came at a terrible price and these attributes did not devolve to many returning soldiers in my generation, but that's how it worked for me.

Beyond that is this simple fact: I must have told myself a hundred times that if I survive Vietnam, I will treat every day for the rest of my life as a gift, a great gift. I did survive and I now have an additional fifty years of those days I consider gifts. Every morning, I wake up in a relatively good mood. I am an optimist. I look forward. I don't dwell on the past. No matter how bad a day might be in my adult life it is indexed against all those terrible days where my very survival was hanging by a thread.

This may be a rub off of the old joke about why are you beating your head against the wall. Remember that one? It feels so good when I stop. You can play tricks on your mind and it can play tricks on you. When I sat down to write a list of all my Vietnam memories I realized I had much better detail recall on the silly incidents and laughable experiences than I did of the actual gut-wrenching ambushes or explosions.

I have a pretty vivid recollection of an afternoon when one of our units was just hanging around at an intersection on Highway One in the Delta three or four miles from our base camp. They radioed in that they wanted the football we often threw around in camp. We could have easily put it on a chopper delivering supplies but we found our own solution.

I made an ambiguous mark on my helmet that might well have been interpreted as a single bar indicating I was a First Lieutenant. We then appropriated a jeep, grabbed the football and drove out of the base camp gates as the guards mistakenly saluted. We were greeted as conquering heroes when we delivered the football. Two guys driving a jeep in an unprotected area in the Delta was quite the shocker.

It all went very smoothly until on our way back we actually came upon a scene where the V.C. had shot up a few South Vietnamese Army vehicles. It was a sobering scene that got even more sobering when we reached for our weapons and realized that in our haste to deliver the football, we had left our rifles on our bunks. Fortunately the incident was over and we made it back unscathed.

But why would I remember this event like it was yesterday but I could barely tell you specific details of ambushes, hot landing zones on helicopter assaults and the like? Your mind weeds out a lot of that negativity particularly when you have tried to put it aside.

And here's a perplexing corollary to all this. I talk about compartmentalizing memories. I talk about denial and lack of communication. I guess the track record speaks for itself on my failure to keep in touch with people from that year of my life. But I can't think of a single day in the last fifty years that Vietnam has not crossed my mind. There's always something that connects to it. It's always there. Vietnam is something I tried to hide from myself and everyone else and yet it is clearly a cornerstone of my identity. If I have learned nothing more from writing all this, it is that. I am and have been shaped by an experience I have spent a lifetime trying to tuck away.

Still, the bottom line is that each day is a gift. Not just a gift but a cherished gift. Today is an example. I am writing at the kitchen table. My wife is chatting from the other room. We're setting up a trip to New York to see two of our daughters. We walked the dogs in light rain a little while ago. This may sound mundane and boring to many but it's a stress free morning to me. And my mindset is that the day will get better. I don't know how just yet but I always look forward to something good on the horizon. Good things that will always be a counterweight to the baggage of the past.

# 38

# LUCY AND THE LETTERS

I HAVE SHARED LITTLE SNIPPETS about my mother along the way knowing that I faced the daunting task of describing her more fully here at the end. It's okay to call her Lucy now since that's what I called her in our thirty some post-Vietnam years.

She was a study in contradictions. Lucy could be charming and engaged and at times equally exasperating. She was opinionated and funny but she could also be petty and even a little cruel at times. She could cut through bullshit like a meat cleaver. Lucy was quick with a smile but even quicker with a zinger.

One of my favorite stories about her was when I took a girl-friend I dating at the time to meet her for the first time. Keep in mind I told her virtually nothing about my personal life in my twenties and thirties because she had a tendency to pry. At any rate, we arrived at her house and I was pleased upon my instant inspection that Lucy was sober. That didn't mean she wasn't loaded for bear.

"So Lauren," she said sweetly after a brief introduction. "My son says if he wants dinner he has two choices. He can make himself a sandwich or take you to an expensive restaurant."

I may have implied something like this but her saying it did not get the visit off to a smooth start.

Lucy's background was filled with contradictions as well. She had grown up extremely poor in a small town in Oregon supported by a single mother. But her mother had grown up in a well to do Kentucky family before she ran off with what would have been termed in those days an "inappropriate man," my grandfather, who later left her with four kids.

Some of her Kentucky relatives were interesting people that she never knew. Her uncle Robley Feland was a top executive at BBDO Advertising in the 1930's and 1940's. He wrote something called "The Mr. Brown Letter" which is still studied in advertising schools today.

I mentioned Charley McDowell who was her newspaper cousin at the *Richmond Times* but there was another I believe second cousin none of us knew but who was an interesting if not famous movie director. He was Paul Bartell and his wild sex comedy film was called *Eating Raoul*.

Maybe it was in that spirit of comedy that Lucy left a message for me at work one day. I walked into the newsroom at KING-TV in Seattle where I was working as a reporter and three of my female colleagues all but leapt on me hissing for me to call my mother.

"She says you haven't called her for six months!" said one.

"What kind of horrible son are you?" asked another.

Heck, we lived in the same city. I could barely escape her phone calls. I had spoken with her the day before but if Lucy wanted something, and I'm sure she did, she had all manner of ways to get your attention. This was just one of the more creative ones. I think those women in the newsroom still think I'm a heel.

But for all her complications and outrageous behavior Lucy was there for me when I needed her. When I read back now over the letters it is clear to me that in Vietnam I just needed a plain old mom and she became just that for the year. She kept a steady stream of letters coming to me and responded as best she could to my demands for food and books. And let's not forget she went to great lengths to help me get home a little early.

I tried to keep my letters to her light and filled with my not so subtle attempts at humor. I did not want to upset her unnecessarily. Her letters in return shielded me in some ways as well. She never spoke of her worries which had to have been monumental. She simply did what she could to make my life easier. And while we got along reasonably well after Vietnam I have to say that this had been an exceptional time in our lives. Without even discussing it, we felt our way through unfamiliar roles and conquered adversity together.

Late in life Lucy was proud to live independently in her own downtown Seattle apartment. She refused things like Meals on Wheels and other senior help. We were living in Seattle at the time and my wife took our young kids to see her pretty regularly. She died at 87 in 2001. She had taken a walk to the liquor store that morning and was waiting for her new computer to arrive when we believe her heart simply failed. Sharp to the very end, she had vowed to take on the Internet.

My sister Kathy packed up Lucy's apartment and moved all the Vietnam letters back to Oregon where they sat for another fifteen years.

I think in retrospect Lucy had kept the letters because she recognized Vietnam as a uniquely shared time in our lives, something that never even occurred to me until I started on this project. She had provided me with a written legacy I could share with my family. It has been an odd experience reliving history through my own twenty year old eyes but I'm pretty sure what I have done here would have made Lucy happy. If I had known about the letters earlier I might have teased her for packing all that old junk around. Now, it just seems much more fitting to say, "Thanks, Mom."